architecture

Tony Chapman

architecture

99

The RIBA Awards

••• ellipsis

All rights reserved. No part of this publication may be reproduced in any form without the prior permission of the copyright holder

First published 1999 by ●●●ellipsis

© 1999 The Royal Institute of British Architects

ISBN 1 84166 045 0

CATALOGUING IN PUBLICATION
A CIP record for this book is available from the British Library

Printed in Great Britain by Service Point

ORDERING INFORMATION
ellipsis london limited
2 Rufus Street, London N1 6PE
T 020 7739 3157
F 020 7739 3175
E sales@ellipsis.co.uk
www.ellipsis.com

Contents

Judging the Stirling Prize	6
The Stirling Prize	13
The Stephen Lawrence Prize	23
Client of the Year	27
Category Award Winners	31
RIBA Awards	69
Assessors	169
Sponsors	171
The Stephen Lawrence Trust	173
Picture Credits	175

Judging the Stirling Prize

'Don't you ever stop talking about architecture?' asked the fashion designer Stella McCartney, one of the five Stirling Prize judges, as we trailed round London, then Oxfordshire, Germany, Dublin and finally Scotland, to find this year's winner. With only three days to reach such a momentous decision, discussion is pretty nonstop and takes place in the most unlikely places – queuing for a taxi at Heathrow Airport, on the plane, at breakfast, and finally, and crucially, around the table at the RIBA.

The initial issue or conundrum, especially for those who were new to the judging experience, was how to choose from such a disparate list of buildings when we were forced to close our ears to tales of lavish budgets or savage cost-cutting, and instead had to focus on the 'the architect whose building has made the greatest contribution to British architecture in the past year'. One thing we could agree on is that this year's shortlist was exceptionally strong, although the buildings, as usual, were so different in scale that even one of the more seasoned judges moaned that the task ahead was 'almost impossible'.

It was also proving impossible to predict a winner. This year, the *Sunday Telegraph* took a gamble and proclaimed that the Lord's Media Stand would battle it out against the Reichstag in Berlin and North Greenwich Jubilee Line Extension station. Right so far, but the paper threw in a couple of wild cards which, from our perspective, was all to the good. Awards must generate gossip but, more importantly, debate. The Booker and Turner Prizes both do admirably well on this score, but architecture poses particular problems in generating media attention and public involvement.

This is partly, I suspect, because the RIBA awards system is seen as an annual display of mutual self-congratulation, which only recognises buildings in the established style. Lack of public involvement (despite a Stirling Prize website) may also be explained by the relative inaccessibility of the shortlisted buildings. The Lord's Media Stand is in a professional enclave, the Reichstag and the Sto headquarters are both in Germany, Ranelagh primary school is on the outskirts of Dublin. True, two of the buildings are stations on the new JLE, but are still relative newcomers (North Greenwich has been open for less than two months.) Only the River and Rowing Museum in Henley was a truly public building.

There was one significant omission from the initial shortlist: the Museum of Scotland in Edinburgh. Although the RIBA panel for Scotland had failed to recommend it for a category award, I, for one, felt it had been overlooked – possibly because it was being judged on style grounds and not being seen in the broader context of a major piece of architecture. For this reason it was 'called in' – similar in some ways to the decision last year to call in the British Library – though the outcome, as it transpired, was rather different.

The judges were Michael Manser, chairman of the RIBA Awards panel; RIBA president Marco Goldschmied; Rick Mather, runner-up in last year's Stirling Prize for the Stein House in Hampstead; myself as editor of the RIBA Journal, the sponsor of the prize; and Stella McCartney. The itinerary, planned with military precision by Nancy Mills of the RIBA Awards office, began at Waterloo station at 9 am one weekday morning and ended, some 57 hours later, on the 18.05 pm flight back from Edinburgh.

At Waterloo, we picked up the Jubilee Line Extension to Stratford station, by Chris Wilkinson Architects, where we were met by the JLE's Roland Paoletti, 1998's RIBA Client of the Year. A rule of the Stirling Prize is that the architect is not allowed to take the jury around their building – it's felt that it stops the judges having full and frank discussions while walking round, and that architects, with their long experience of presenting to clients, can try to sell their building too hard.

As it turned out, Stratford needed no selling. This, we felt, was due partly to the simplicity of the single, dramatic linear space, which is so strong one hardly notices that a train line cuts through the middle of it. It is also because the connections between the three train lines at the station (the JLE, Central and North London Lines) are refreshingly straightforward, making orientation through the building a joy.

Back on the JLE (still working like a dream) to Alsop Lyall & Störmer's North Greenwich station – an awesome blue cave that couldn't fail to impress even those among us whose taste is more austere. A debate ensued about the colour, an intense cobalt blue: would it look dated in ten years? There was disagreement, but I thought not. The heroic scale and simple elegance of the civil-engineering structure are strong enough to stand the test of time – the colour, something of an Alsop signature – divides it from the rest of the JLE, which is more sombre. Yet North Greenwich failed to win us over in quite the way that Stratford station had. Some felt that, spatially, it was not as dramatic as had been promised by the drawings and that it lacked the clarity of its rival.

Moving from these two examples of very public architecture to Future Systems' Lord's Media Centre, sponsored by NatWest, highlights why Stirling judges have a hard time. We'd agreed that the JLE stations will improve the lot of Londoners – which on its own must be worth a few votes – yet here we were at the world's most famous cricket club, looking at a building that is fully used only six months a year – and then only by journalists.

To Future Systems, the building's significance resides in it being the first aluminium semi-monocoque building in the world. To the judges, that was less important than its ability to lift the spirits and the fact that it is so unexpected, a complete one-off, an icon which recasts cricket in a futuristic light. We were smitten.

Judging the Stirling Prize

Back on the minibus and out on the M4 to David Chipperfield Architects' River and Rowing Museum at Henley-on-Thames. It's a building we were curious to see; it has already picked up its fair share of awards, including a RIBA Award in 1998 and the RFAC Building of the Year this year.

There was a mixed reaction. We had no doubts that the architect had had a difficult job trying to satisfy the demands of a conservative client and the building's setting, right on the river. However, we could not see why (apart from the obvious references to traditional boathouses), the main space had been designed with two pitched roofs, with the result that the exhibition area had to be used vertically. Also, we were unsure about the later addition, which was a more conventional box and did not have the simple elegance of the earlier building.

Then to Berlin and for some of us the highlight of the three days – Foster & Partners' Reichstag. I had already toured the building in the summer and on that visit had been struck by the queues of tourists. While the politicians' areas – the plenary chamber, committee rooms, party offices, bars and restaurants – were deserted, the public spaces were humming. It was no different this time. The public areas, which include one small restaurant, are not generous enough to cope with the number of visitors, suggesting that the client has misjudged the building's popularity.

In addition, the great glazed cupola, the only exclusively public area, plays a purely symbolic rather than functional role. Like most visitors, I had assumed that from the roof one could look down on MPs in the chamber; in fact, the internal views are restricted and all one can do is gaze out over the new Berlin.

This is not to say we were disappointed: the Reichstag is surely one of the most spectacular visitor experiences in Europe. However, some of us felt that its success lies not so much with Foster's attempt to create a powerful symbol of popular democracy, but with the skill with which the practice has used modern materials and technology to bring the German parliament building back to life.

Still in Germany, Michael Wilford & Partners' headquarters building for Sto was praised for the way in which it heralded a newer, clear corporate image for the building-products company. But we were less convinced by the building's relationship to the topography of the site. It was recognised that some of the issues – for example, the disparity between the new building and the company's existing studio – would be resolved when the masterplan for the whole site is carried through. Nevertheless, we didn't feel it was going to make the final three.

With two projects to be visited on the third and final day, the strain was definitely beginning to show. Could we face another building and another tour? Bleary-eyed, we assembled at Heathrow Airport for an early morning flight to Dublin to see O'Donnell & Tuomey's Ranelagh primary school, a striking piece of new architecture in a suburb of the city – and the rank outsider on the shortlist, but one which fully deserved to be there. We particularly liked the way in which the architect had strived to make spaces that were neither typical nor overtly special – corridors, for example, that are wide enough to be used as teaching spaces – which succeed in promising a great variety of spatial experiences.

And, finally, to Edinburgh, to see the new Museum of Scotland, by Benson & Forsyth, commissioned in those far-off pre-lottery days through the competition system – and which had narrowly missed being scalped by the Prince of Wales and others who had criticised the jury's decision to give the commission to a non-traditional practice. It would be interesting to know what HRH thinks now the building is complete. Of all the shortlisted entries, this was the one that exercised us the most.

Those who love it do so for the very reasons that its detractors find it hard to accept, namely its complexity: the woven space and volumes, and the marriage between the building and the exhibits.

Externally, the building has great civic presence, overpowering, it has to be said, the original museum but sitting comfortably in this part of Edinburgh. Architecturally, we all felt, it was a conundrum: old-fashioned in some ways but a building deeply rooted in the modernist tradition, and one that had the greatest resonance with Jim Stirling's work.

Despite the nonstop talking, no one seemed sure they had reached a decision. 'Sleep on it', someone advised and so we did, to reassemble in Marco Goldschmied's office at the RIBA the following day. Low-key would sum up the mood of the discussion, which led to us narrowing the list down to the final three. The buildings we wanted to discuss further were: the Lord's Media Centre, Stratford JLE station and the Museum of Scotland. Then the choice narrowed to just two – everyone admired Stratford greatly but no one was prepared to be passionate about it. Despite a bad beginning, the Museum of Scotland was, we agreed, an extraordinary building, but some felt that being so architecturally specific, it could create difficulties for future curators. Others on the jury felt that the complexity, particularly internally, is taken to excess.

The Media Centre won because, in the end, we felt it was the building that sums up 1999, and a building that would have been unthinkable in the 1980s. It is a highly fashionable structure with its amorphous shapes and 'retro futurist feel', but it amounts to more than that. It brings a breath of fresh air to the language and form of the modern movement. The technology and construction methods used might not filter through to the architecture of the coming millennium, but then again, they just might.
AMANDA BAILLIEU editor, RIBA *Journal*

The Stirling Prize

The Stirling Prize is given for the RIBA Building of the Year. It is sponsored by the *RIBA Journal* and is presented to the architects of the building which has made the greatest contribution to British architecture in the past year. The winning architect receives a cash prize of £20,000.

The prize is named after the great British architect Sir James Stirling. (1926–92), one of the most important British architects of his generation and a progressive thinker and designer throughout his career. He was a major influence on architects as diverse as Richard Rogers and Leon Krier.

NatWest Media Centre, Lord's Cricket Ground

Digital alarm clock, bar-code reader, alien starship: these are a few of the press's attempts to convey an impression of a structure that may at first have seemed alien to its very conventional setting. But this is Lord's, which contains some of the best examples of modern architecture in London – and already the Media Centre is accepted as part of the summer scene.

Future Systems recognised the 'eternal and sacred' atmosphere of the ground in their competition entry, yet they have come up with a structure that is entirely new. As a media centre, it is both the medium and the message. Its soft lines, not least in its less-photographed back, reflect its origins in a Cornish boatyard but also mirror the sweeping curves of the stands. It is the world's first all-aluminium semi-monocoque building, using the technique of welding the skin on to a structure of ribs and spars, characteristic of boat and aircraft building and obviating the need for obstructive columns. Internally, it is as comfortable and luxurious as the 50s Chevrolet whose baby-blue upholstery inspired it. It hovers 15 metres above the ground, providing perfect all-round views for journalists and allowing access to the Nursery Ground beyond. It faces due west, hence the need for comfort cooling, partly in the form of the kind of individual blowers older passenger jets use. External glare, which has stopped cricket matches elsewhere, is avoided by tilting the window through 25 degrees.

JURY COMMENT The NatWest Media Centre has become an instant icon. A large white eye on the world of cricket, it communicates the MCC's belief in the future of the game and contrasts almost irreverently with the traditional pavilion it faces. The simple design clearly communicates its purpose and imposes itself on this historic arena, thus avoiding the risk of becoming just another charm on the Lord's bracelet. The structure suggests a new world of off-site manufacturing and a level of consistent

Future Systems

NatWest Media Centre, Lord's Cricket Ground   15

The Stirling Prize

Future Systems

NatWest Media Centre, Lord's Cricket Ground

quality that (sadly) is more associated with the car industry. One of the most impressive aspects of the design is the way it neatly avoids the age-old problems of scale, mass and context, which traditional forms find difficult to transcend. These issues just do not apply to its sleek form. Concern has been expressed about the complexities of maintaining such a building, but it must be remembered that it is only used for part of the year and can be cleaned prior to each match, ensuring that it retains its new, crisp, white appearance.

The Stirling Prize judges said, 'The NatWest Media Centre is already a TV personality. It is its own thing, completely unusual and totally uncompromising. It is a breath of architectural fresh air. Perhaps that is why we all got so excited as we walked into the Media Centre. Judges try to put themselves into the position of an eight-year-old when they first see a building, and this was the one, we all agreed, as eight-year-olds we would have the most fun in. In fact everyone felt ten years younger, seeing the blue.

'It is a complete one-off: a wacky solution to a singular problem. There is something brilliant about having a dream and seeing it through. Future Systems have been wanting to do this for a long time and they've done it. In so many ways this is the building of 1999: an extraordinary iconic structure that has landed in the middle of Lord's and changed the face of cricket. It is at last the 20th century – in the nick of time. It may or may not be the future but it certainly works.'

ADDRESS London NW8
CLIENT Marylebone Cricket Club
CONTRACTOR Pendennis Shipyard
STRUCTURE Ove Arup & Partners
CONTRACT VALUE £5 million

Future Systems

NatWest Media Centre, Lord's Cricket Ground 17

The Stirling Prize

Future Systems

The Museum of Scotland

The Museum of Scotland is a public building of enormous significance for the city and the country, not least in that its completion has coincided with Scotland regaining a greater degree of independence than at any time in the past three centuries. Externally the building makes a strong contemporary statement while remaining rooted in the vernacular of the capital city. The simplicity of its forms – the rectangular exhibition block, the cylindrical tower, the curved cantilevered light-reflecting roof terrace – are all given an urban texture with the stone banding, the slitted windows and by the bridges that link all the elements.

The building seeks to be rigorously contextual, defined as it is by the façades around it. The museum responds dynamically by reinforcing or subverting the existing street pattern. The tower forms a hinge between the north and west façades, acting as a focal point at the convergence of five routes into the city. The height of the perimeter galleries respects the height of the buildings to the north, while elements along Bristo Port reflect the asymmetry of the smaller-scale buildings to the south. Meanwhile the core gallery rises like a castle keep through the curtain wall. Although it did not receive a Category Award, the Museum was shortlisted for the Stirling Prize.

JURY COMMENT The deliberate addition of complexity to a fundamentally simple plan, particularly internally, is at times taken to excess, leaving the building flawed. But in the final analysis the integration of a building of this kind into its urban context and the creation of a new landmark for Edinburgh, a city which already contains much of the physical heritage of Scotland, represents a considerable architectural achievement. In the context of this dramatic city, it makes a strong and contemporary statement – the simplicity of the external

Benson and Forsyth Architects

The Museum of Scotland

Stirling Prize runner-up

Benson and Forsyth Architects

The Museum of Scotland

forms create an urban impact on this site, generating a series of changing views and glimpses from all around the city. The interior spaces are dramatic and befitting a public museum of this importance and the attention with which each exhibit has been located and displayed deserves special note.

Stirling Prize runner up

ADDRESS Chambers Street, Edinburgh
CLIENT Trustees of the National Museums of Scotland
MANAGEMENT CONTRACTOR Bovis Construction (Scotland) Ltd
STRUCTURE Antony Hunt Associates
CONTRACT VALUE £44,850,000

Benson and Forsyth Architects

The Museum of Scotland 21

Stirling Prize runner-up

Benson and Forsyth Architects

The Stephen Lawrence Prize

The Stephen Lawrence Prize, sponsored by the Goldschmied Trust, is intended to give greater prominence to the creativity demonstrated on smaller projects. It is awarded to the architect of an RIBA Award-winning building costing less than £500,000. The Prize, introduced in 1998, commemorates Stephen Lawrence, the black teenager planning to become an architect who was murdered in south London in 1993, and supports the charitable trust set up in his name. The winning architect receives £5000. Last year the winner was Ian Ritchie for his Cultural Greenhouse at Terrasson in south-west France.

This year a shortlist of four was chosen from among the RIBA Award winners: Beetham House, a home for young people with behavioural difficulties, by Houlton Taylor Architects; Market Lane Public Conveniences, a reworking of a 1950s municipal toilet by architecture plb; the Sculpture Gallery at Roche Court, Wiltshire, attached to a Grade-II* listed building, by Munkenbeck and Marshall; and Skywood House, a private house built on a newly created lake in Denham by Graham Phillips.

The winner of the 1999 Stephen Lawrence Prize is the Sculpture Gallery at Roche Court. The runner-up is Beetham House.

Sculpture Gallery, New Art Centre

Roche Court is a Grade II* listed building constructed for Lord Nelson in 1806. The setting is used as a sculpture park containing works by the most famous sculptors of the century, including Anthony Gormley, Allen Jones and Barbara Hepworth. The brief was to build a sculpture gallery against the kitchen garden wall that runs between the house and the orangery. This is a working gallery, not a museum: all the art is for sale.

JURY COMMENT The solution devised by the architects has produced a sublime essay in calm modernism, happy in its historic context. The clever cross-section in both directions results in a roof which is as visually light as possible. Although a small project, this is Architecture with a big A. The client is also to be applauded for her insight in commissioning sensitive contemporary architecture, when it would have been easy to resort to reproduction or pastiche.

The Stephen Lawrence Prize judges said, 'The Sculpture Gallery cannot be bettered. It is a conjuring trick, conjuring everything out of almost nothing. It feeds and enriches the orangery, moving it closer to the house, fusing the two buildings and making them one whole. The new gallery demonstrates why proportion and quality of execution are the chief criteria in the debate about contextualism. The planning officer is also to be congratulated for his enlightened support.'

ADDRESS Roche Court, East Winterslow, Salisbury, Wiltshire
CLIENT Lady Bessborough
CONTRACTOR Martin Price, Lower Bemerton
STRUCTURE Barton Engineers
CONTRACT VALUE £100,000

Stephen Lawrence Prize

Munkenbeck + Marshall

Sculpture Gallery, New Art Centre   25

Stephen Lawrence Prize

Munkenbeck + Marshall

Client of the Year

All architects realise that a supportive, committed and imaginative client is key to the success of any building. This award is intended to make the general public aware of the importance of such clients in the creation of fine buildings. This award is fully supported by the Architecture: Visual Arts Department of the Arts Council of England. The prize is a work of art, commissioned by the client, to the value of £5000. Last year's Award was made to Roland Paoletti for his role in orchestrating the work of ten commissioned architects and his own in-house team on the Jubilee Line Extension, and was used to commission works of art for the new stations.

Client of the Year 1999 is the Marylebone Cricket Club.

The Marylebone Cricket Club

The MCC has been awarded the Client of the Year Award in recognition of the series of fine buildings which they have commissioned at Lord's, the headquarters of English cricket.

The stimulus for their nomination was of course the Award-winning NatWest Media Centre by Future Systems, but the Award is made in recognition also of a series of exemplary buildings which transformed the charming but faded ground into a stimulating venue in which to watch cricket. Under the imaginative guidance of Peter Bell, Gareth Williams, Mike Blow and the rest of the team, the MCC has commissioned some of the best public architecture in recent years, starting with Michael Hopkins's Mound Stand (1985–7), with its then highly original tented roof. In the mid 1990s they commissioned David Morley to contribute three buildings which won RIBA Awards: an Indoor Cricket School (1996), which features a half-glazed barrel vaulted roof that filters the light through fabric louvres and two 1997 winners: the headquarters of the English Cricket Board, a naturally ventilated metal and opaque glass-clad building, and an exquisite if temporary shop. Nicholas Grimshaw was commissioned to rebuild the Grandstand in 1995. It was completed in 1998. And now, the jewel in the crown, Future Systems' NatWest Media Centre, which this year's judges described as 'an instant icon. A large white eye on the world of cricket, communicating the MCC's belief in the future of the game and contrasting almost irreverently with the traditional pavilion it faces. The simple design clearly communicates its purpose and imposes itself on this historic arena.'

The client's role is central to the process of producing architecture of excellence, and is exemplified by the MCC over the past 15 years.

The Marylebone Cricket Club 29

Client of the Year

Category Award Winners

The Category Awards form the shortlist for the Stirling Prize and are arranged in seven building types: Arts and Leisure, Civic and Community, Commercial, Conservation, Education, Health, and Housing. Since the judges are looking for outstanding examples of that category of building – not just the best of those entered – and for some contribution made to the development of the building type, in any year some categories may have more than one winner, others may have none. This year, sadly, the judges felt unable to give awards in the Health or Housing categories.

The River and Rowing Museum Mill

With its pitched roof, the River and Rowing Museum makes reference to the traditional wooden barns and boat houses of Henley; the rest is all invention. Its transparent, open ground floor accommodates café, shop, small galleries and meeting rooms; the first-floor boat-halls float above, comprising closed boxes of oak lit only by ridged skylights, and housing the main exhibition spaces. The building sits on a new raised ground plane which extends around it, like the platform round a Japanese temple.

The design is both a response to a conservative planning environment which resisted any departure from comprehensible form, and to a local fear of new building per se. By combining the local vernacular with the ambitious manipulation of space and light, Chipperfield has produced a building which local people seem to like, despite their fears.

JURY COMMENT This quite complex building leaves one with a memory of simplicity. The shell of the building and its contents are articulated with an intense clarity. The form was intended to recall upturned boats and this really is the case, with the solid mass of oak-clad floor and the steeply sloping terned stainless-steel roof floating hull-like upside down over the glass-enclosed ground floor. From both the tow-path and the rear car park, you can see light and landscape beyond.

While the container is detailed with great clarity, the exhibition display (by other hands) is less so. In particular, in one of the two upper galleries where the design of the suspension for the boats on display is clumsy and heavy. Fortunately the other gallery has been left more or less as built, a stunning high white space of pointed section, though even here long views are impeded by a (worthy) area designed for children. The circulation and the various ancillary areas are elegantly functional – there is a particularly beautiful lift. And the restaurant – which oddly does not face the

David Chipperfield Architects

The River and Rowing Museum Mill 33

David Chipperfield Architects

Arts and leisure

The River and Rowing Museum Mill

river – is a peaceful place. The flat-roofed annexe, approached via an elegant glazed bridge which maps the route of the Thames, disappoints by comparison. The space is dark, almost claustrophobic and externally its shape fights the rest of the building. Overall though, the museum perfectly gathers the sense of the peaceful riverside. As the lay representative thought, the building gives an impression of always having been there – not deferentially but boldly.

ADDRESS Mill Meadows, Henley on Thames, Oxon
CLIENT The River and Rowing Museum Foundation
CONTRACTOR Norwest Holst Construction Ltd
STRUCTURE Whitby Bird & Partners
CONTRACT VALUE £6 million

David Chipperfield Architects

The River and Rowing Museum Mill   35

Arts and leisure

David Chipperfield Architects

North Greenwich Station

North Greenwich Station, built to begin the long-term regeneration of the derelict peninsula, immediately acted as the catalyst for the choice of site for the Millennium Dome. By Alsop Lyall & Störmer to construction tender stage, it was completed over several years by one of Roland Paoletti's Jubilee Line Extension project teams. The collaboration has produced one of the most efficient, free-spirited and poetic stations on the line, spectacular in the scale of its ambition and achievement.

When the dome opens it will handle 120,000 passengers an hour. The simple-hall-like arrangement gives it the spatial clarity of the major public building it is. From Foster's cool, elegant, white transport interchange which sits on top, the passenger descends past walls of blue glass, vivid with real cobalt, to a wide deck level suspended in space, with the tracks visible below on either side. More escalators lead down to the platform-level concourse. Here glass doors slide apart as the train arrives and its doors open. This safety device also adds drama to the occasion of catching a tube. The void looks staggering but the public areas at North Greenwich are no bigger than those at any other underground station – it is simply the powerful effect of good architecture at work in opening it up. Ultramarine blue mosaic tiles clad the v-shaped columns and walls, with a paler blue terrazzo on the floor.

JURY COMMENT The scale is boldly declared in the open layout of the station, such that an initial visit is almost shocking in its intensity, at the same time as being immensely pleasing. The ambition of the new JLE stations has surely not been seen in London's public transport since Charles Holden's stations in the 1930s. It's worth a trip on the Underground just to see it, but this station should brighten the travel of any commuter.

Alsop Lyall & Störmer with JLE Project Team

North Greenwich Station 37

Civic and Community

Alsop Lyall & Störmer with JLE Project Team

38 **North Greenwich Station**

Later judges said: 'Grand in scale, North Greenwich station is essentially about drama. Although it has already become famous as the 'blue station', its power comes from the soaring spaces, changing levels and exposed vertical circulation. Glass side panels allow passengers to look at the platforms below, enhancing the feeling of space. Once down on platform level there are exciting vertiginous views back up to concourse level. The feeling of being in a subterranean cavern – far from being unpleasant – is almost other-worldly, and is enhanced by the use of ultramarine blue on the walls, floors and ceiling. The bigger issue here is that, despite the restrictions imposed by the client, the architect has managed to turn what is normally a humdrum experience (waiting for a tube) into something very special.' Another judge likened it to Alsop's 1997 category-winning municipal building in Marseilles: 'Like a Grand-Bleu turned inside out.'

The judges also cited the view of the owner-operator, Ron Delaney, 'At North Greenwich, lines of sight are as clear as day, machines are recessed into walls and there is ample space for customer circulation. North Greenwich is about dignified stress-free travel for passengers and a pleasant work environment for staff. From its brilliantly lit and spacious ticket hall, the passenger passes into the calming blue and equally generous proportions of the station's sub-surface interior. There is no oppressive feeling of being underground: although it is dark, it is 'light'. This is a big departure from the catacomb experience of conventional Underground space.'

ADDRESS London SE10
CLIENT London Underground Limited
CONTRACTOR McAlpine-Wayss & Freylag
STRUCTURE Benaim Works Joint Venture
CONTRACT VALUE £110 million

Alsop Lyall & Störmer with JLE Project Team

North Greenwich Station 39

Alsop Lyall & Störmer with JLE Project Team

Stratford Regional Station

Stratford Station is a focal point for the regeneration of the Borough of Newham. As such, its ambitions are far greater than just making the process of changing trains quicker and simpler though it achieves both these aims supremely well. A mass of railway lines with completely different track orientations meet and cross here: one practical reason for the grand civic scale of this building. The station has an airport glamour about it but like an airport, it also has to be functional. A concrete subway under all the lines and a series of connecting stairs and escalators make interchange logical and straightforward. The space is formed by a cantilevered curved shell steel envelope enclosed along its long edge and ends with structural glass walls.

JURY COMMENT The geometry of the interior is effortless, allowing the rectangle of the main shell to control the varying angles produced by the relationship to the railway lines, with a deft lightness of touch. The whole building is impeccably detailed. There is a sense that real experience-in-depth has been brought to bear on the handling and manufacture of all the elements. The result is a dramatic enclosure, all the more so in the context of Stratford. By day it is an evident grand new public space and by night the lit underside of the shell transforms the structure into a gigantic light sculpture. We were genuinely in awe of the whole building.'

Later judges had this to say: 'Essentially this is one huge curved shell of a canopy that swings up from the edge of the tracks and arches over the ticket hall, gates and the other paraphernalia of modern railways. The necessary enclosure is completed by a delicately detailed glazing that does not prevent the shell from seemingly gathering the exterior space of the plaza to itself. The impact on the exterior urban space is profound, as evidenced by conversations with passers-by who really appeared to feel

Chris Wilkinson Architects

Stratford Regional Station 41

Civic and community

Chris Wilkinson Architects

Stratford Regional Station

that the station had ennobled their bit of the town. We had a reservation about the interior planning – there are many 'gash' spaces on display, the first floor feels especially empty at present but this should be ameliorated when the station is fully occupied with – we would hope – well-designed franchises.'

They cited the client as saying, 'This extraordinary form-meets-function building not only sets exemplary standards in public architecture but is a highly visible landmark within the local environment (never mind a landmark building for London Underground). The mere sight of this extraordinary building puts a spring into the step and sends out a message of hope to those living in or passing through this borough-with-a-future.'

ADDRESS London E15
CLIENT Jubilee Line Extension Project, London Underground Ltd
CONTRACTOR Kvaerner Construction
STRUCTURE Hyder Consulting Ltd
CONTRACT VALUE £17 million

Chris Wilkinson Architects

Stratford Regional Station 43

Civic and community

Chris Wilkinson Architects

Sto AG Marketing and Training Building

The Sto building announces itself to the world and to its village setting, close to the Swiss border, not only through the bold company logo on its roof but through the dramatic parallelogram shape of its cantilevered four-storey office block. This sits above a two-storey square base housing training facilities, connected to it by an oval entrance pavilion. The idea of building-as-statement is carried through in the use of the company's products throughout: the office block is surfaced with an insulated stucco system; curved blue metal panels are used in the opaque half of the reception oval; and the lower walls are clad in square panels of grey basalt, with contrasting panels of coloured enamel.

The reception area is a riot of colour, using Sto turquoise, orange and mauve finishes. Floors too show off company products. The building also makes reference to naval architecture: the office block, with its blunt bows and stepped balconies at the stern, floats elegantly in the valley. These balconies provide sun decks for staff, with superb views of mountains and forest. The basement area, used for practical training in product use, is lit by continuous high windows and by the peeling away of a section of the pavilion floor above. At ground-floor level, seminar rooms have flexible partitions and overlook a garden. An open well next to the stair allows light to flood through the building and provides views between levels.

JURY COMMENT This is a truly remarkable building both in and out of its context. Already the Sto company dominates this small Alpine village and it is planned to grow still further. This is a company town and the Sto logo shouts the fact from the rooftops at the passing traffic in vivid yellow lettering and in a way that could never happen in the UK. The lack of reticence in this setting could have been appalling, had this been a less good building. In fact its very boldness shows that good design can

Michael Wilford & Partners

Sto AG Marketing and Training Building 45

Commercial

Michael Wilford & Partners

46   Sto AG Marketing and Training Building

transcend the need for a contextual approach. The striking geometry of the envelope is matched by the colourful brilliance of the interior which, like the outside, acts as an advertising hoarding, with the clashing use of Sto finishes. The interior is tight, particularly in corridors and stairwells, but the apparently accidental juxtapositions of space and form are developed and organised to dramatic effect particularly in the foyer and at lower ground-floor level, where the ovoid shafts would tempt any child or perhaps any visitor to crawl.

The exterior use of colour is perhaps less successful – already the mauve is beginning to fade in the southern sun as it has at the Staatsgallerie in Stuttgart. With that one reservation aside, this is indeed a scheme that builds on the successful relationship between Wilford and Sto.

ADDRESS Stühlingen, Germany
CLIENT Sto AG
CONTRACTOR Züblin AG Freiburg
STRUCTURE Boll and Partner
CONTRACT VALUE DM 15 million

Michael Wilford & Partners

Sto AG Marketing and Training Building 47

Commercial

Michael Wilford & Partners

The Reichstag

Foster and Partners won the commission to rebuild the Reichstag and create a new home for the German Parliament in Berlin, following an open competition. The practice decided to make the building a living museum of German history as well as a working parliament and a highly energy-conscious building.

The poor 1960s accretions were removed, revealing the clarity of the original design, opening up interior courtyards and reinstating the ceremonial entrance as a democratic point of entry for politicians and public alike. The same philosophy is repeated throughout, with the public becoming a part of the process: practically, by paying for the maintenance of the building through the marks they spend in the café on the roof; symbolically by means of the elevated viewing platform, reached by helical ramps, from where they look down on their representatives in the chamber below. The ramps wind round a beehive structure that is a key part of the green strategy of the building, containing energy-supplying photovoltaic cells. This design also reflects daylight into the chamber and effects the removal of hot air as a part of the natural ventilation system. This is the first major public building to be powered by renewable resources – sunflower or rape seed oil – which helps reduce carbon dioxide emissions. Solar power provides lighting. Water is from an artesian well deep below the building and brown water is collected from the roofs for use in the lavatories.

JURY COMMENT We were particularly impressed by the way in which Foster confronts the sense of history that pervades the building, not least in preserving the graffiti of the Russian soldiers who occupied the building in 1945. He exposes the past plainly and simply and in doing so, exposes the visitor to the enormity of Germany's transformation over the

Foster and Partners

The Reichstag 49

Conservation

Foster and Partners

The Reichstag

last fifty years. The history of the building is somehow entwined in this new symbol of democracy and the design subtly balances thoughts of the past with a vision of the future.

The peeling away of the various layers added in the 1950s and 1960s to obscure the original building and intended to deny its existence, has created a unique sense of the building's endurance, which contrasts strikingly with the limited and controlled use of modern materials and technology. This is perhaps the most impressive thing about the quality of the design. A symbiotic relationship. No tricks. The old and new together in a harmony that celebrates a better future without forgetting the past. It is a building that heralds the rebirth of a nation.

ADDRESS Berlin, Germany
CLIENT Bundesbaugesellschaft Berlin mbH
CONTRACTOR Büro am Lützowplatz
STRUCTURE Ove Arup & Partners
CONTRACT VALUE £265 million

Foster and Partners

The Reichstag

Conservation

Foster and Partners

Ranelagh Multi-Denominational School

The agglomeration of buildings that formed the old school produced the starting point for the design of the new. The existing ridgeline of the tin church was used as the height limit for the new building and the line of its north wall set the distance of the new building line from the Georgian terrace behind. The old railings were also preserved and used to enclose a landscaped play area between the school and the terrace. The pitched roofs and first-floor walkway also refer back to the old buildings, but with a distinctly modern spin added. The cladding is timber and the roofs finished in terne-coated steel which weathers to look like lead. The street elevation is quite different. It is broken into two-storey blocks of paired classrooms with a single-storey link between them, topped by a small roof terrace. These and the entry porch are faced with stone taken from an old boundary wall, while reclaimed brick is used for the rest of the main façade and end elevations.

JURY COMMENT We were shocked by how good this project was (it is not easily photographed, even by a top architectural photographer). Considering the initial array of objectors, the design is brave, not least because the architects both have children at the school. (This is the second design, the first by the education department's own architects was refused after hostile local reaction). Our only reservation concerned the panels of random stone on the street elevation. Otherwise the exterior perfectly expressed its internal function in a quiet restrained way. Inside the spaces are delightful, combining the subtle use of exposed concrete, unpainted timber and painted blockwork. The colour scheme is varied and clearly very successful for a primary school. One passer-by commented on how lovely it was: 'So much nicer than the old tin shacks.'

The client, Principal Joan Whelan, is reported as having overheard a

O'Donnell and Tuomey

Ranelagh Multi-Denominational School 53

Education

O'Donnell and Tuomey

conversation between two children passing the school. 'One said, "You see that new building there?" The other guy said, "Yeah, what is it?" The first one said, "That's my school." His friend said, "That can't be a school." "It is," the other insisted. The second kid looked at it again and nodded, "That's a cool school."'

ADDRESS Dublin, Ireland
CLIENT Ranelagh Multi-Denominational School
CONTRACTOR Pierce Healy Developments Ltd, Co Kilkenny
STRUCTURE Fearon O'Neil Rooney
CONTRACT VALUE IR£1,160,000

O'Donnell and Tuomey

Ranelagh Multi-Denominational School 55

Education

O'Donnell and Tuomey

RIBA Awards

RIBA Awards are given for excellence rather than size or complexity. In fact, jurors are urged to include buildings that are otherwise unlikely to come to public notice. Awards are judged regionally by a panel consisting of an architect of national renown (not from that region), a local architect, and a lay person.

Chequer Mead Arts Centre and Theatre

Arts buildings must be accessible – in all senses – to satisfy Arts Council Lottery Fund criteria, as this one did. This was one of the first lottery-funded projects to be completed, with £680,000 provided by the Arts Council and the balance coming from the town and district councils.

The scheme is in three parts: a converted Victorian school, a new theatre, and a garden. It creates its own sense of mystery, with its rhomboidal shapes, clad in windowless cedar, and set at angles to one another, according to a geometry dictated by the site. A new entrance has been made in the front of the old school with a steel and timber canopy. The gallery space, created out of the old school hall, has a large foyer and a robust café, and benefits from the removal of the suspended ceilings revealing high Victorian ceilings.

The *pièce de resistance* though is the new theatre, an intimate space with a flexible proscenium stage and a horseshoe-shaped auditorium, approached through a glazed walkway from the café, which brings audience and performers close together. The dark-blue colour scheme is highlighted by the gold lines of an elegant balcony, giving a sensuous quality to the space.

JURY COMMENT The result is a complex building that succeeds in being at the same time both demanding and approachable and which is well used and appreciated by its client and its public.

ADDRESS De La Warr Road, East Grinstead, West Sussex
CLIENT East Grinstead Town Council
MAIN CONTRACTOR Martin Smith and Foster Ltd
STRUCTURE Harris and Sutherland
CONTRACT VALUE £1,625,000

Tim Ronalds Architects

Chequer Mead Arts Centre and Theatre 59

Arts and leisure

Tim Ronalds Architects

CUBE Gallery

The Centre for the Understanding of the Built Environment (CUBE) has been created in the basement of a Grade II-listed warehouse in the Whitworth conservation area. The design peels away insensitive additions, leaving a series of interconnected galleries, delineated by stark white walls articulated from their background of brick, timber and cast iron. The result is a balanced composition: the warm vernacular of the old warehouse and the new uncluttered surfaces providing a flexible backdrop for exhibitions. High-quality durable finishes are used in the entrance area, stairs and disabled access platform, and on the frameless glazed screens. Other areas have been detailed with a ruthless simplicity, with exposed joists and services. Gallery 1, on the ground floor, uses hinged wall panels that control the degree of diffuse light via etched glass to a retained light well. Light is introduced to Gallery 2 by glazing over at first-floor level. A new staircase of lacquered shot-blasted folded steel descends to Gallery 3 and a seminar room.

JURY COMMENT We were impressed by the easy flow of the gallery; the design is not over-cooked. Maximum use has been made of borrowed space. Even in the basement, vistas through ground level windows and rooflights give contact with the world outside. The Gallery has a friendly versatile character, successfully reconciling the competing demands of a plain backdrop for large exhibitions, with the need for an inviting, intimate venue for public debate.

ADDRESS Portland Street, Manchester
CLIENT Trustees of the CUBE Gallery
CONTRACTOR Curbishley Construction Ltd, Knutsford
STRUCTURE Ove Arup & Partners
CONTRACT VALUE £500,000

Hodder Associates

CUBE Gallery

Arts and leisure

Hodder Associates

The Ikon Gallery

This conversion of a disused school by Birmingham's pre-eminent Victorian practice Martin and Chamberlain, has produced a gallery space that is enjoyed by artists and visitors alike. The Ikon is devoted to showing exhibitions of the works of living artists, with great emphasis placed on education, interpretation and attracting new devotees to contemporary art. The new building reflects these priorities. It has three storeys, with galleries on the first and second floors. There are two staircases and two lifts, one for people, the other for works of art. The building sits on a plinth of slate – the result of involving an artist in the design team – and within a public square which is part of the Brindleyplace redevelopment.

JURY COMMENT It is as if the square pays homage to the quality of this refurbishment: the renovation of the main elevation, the careful rebuilding of the tower (funded with European money), the design of the entrance at the foot of the tower and overall to the elegant reuse of this disused school. Inside, the public spaces appear surprisingly small in relation to the bulk of the building. It is not until you go behind the scenes and see the back-up areas – the school visitor room, storage and so on – that the whole building begins to make sense. The detailing is clear and simple and pays great attention to the artist's uncompromising requirement for no visual intrusions.

ADDRESS Oozells Square, Birmingham
CLIENT Ikon Gallery
CONTRACTOR Tarmac Building, Wolverhampton
STRUCTURE Peel and Fowler
CONTRACT VALUE £4,280,000

Levitt Bernstein

The Ikon Gallery 63

Arts and leisure

Levitt Bernstein

The Landmark

Ilfracombe is a traditional English holiday resort set on the rugged north Devon coast. After the old Victorian Theatre was damaged in a storm in 1990, it was decided to replace it with a 450-seat theatre. Extensive consultation took place before the design was accepted by a show of hands at a huge town meeting. Architecture is now an issue in the town, and has given residents a sense that public initiative can change things.

The most striking features of the design are the two conical structures of white load-bearing bricks. Though dubbed 'Madonna's Bra' by some of the press, they are a serious design solution. Firstly they supply a creative technical response for a building which has to withstand regular battering from the sea and avoid the use of steel in a corrosive environment; secondly they provide dramatic spaces which are clearly successful, judging by the full programmes of public and private functions; thirdly, they announce that this is a building of civic importance. They also present an unusual acoustical challenge for which Arup Acoustics have come up with a solution involving reflective and absorbent panels.

JURY COMMENT As a stand-alone pavilion, it does not need to be polite. And in this rugged context the highly original form fits well, while shouting its existence to the world. It is a credit to all concerned that a bold contemporary and consistent solution has been built, instead of the Victorian pastiche it might so easily have been.

ADDRESS Wilder Road, Ilfracombe, Devon
CLIENT North Devon District Council
CONTRACTOR Pearce Construction (Barnstaple) Ltd
STRUCTURE Harris and Sutherland
CONTRACT VALUE £3.7 million

Tim Ronalds Architects

The Landmark 65

Arts and leisure

Tim Ronalds Architects

New Foyer Gallery

The brief called for a number of solutions: to provide a legible gateway to the Institute of Art and Design; to make the whole complex accessible in the broadest sense; to provide a foyer and meeting space; and to house a sculpture gallery. The existing flank entrance wall has been extended in height, rendered, signed and lit to lead the visitor's eye along it and into the gallery, where it becomes an exhibition wall. The building itself is a simple fully-glazed pavilion. The lightweight steel-and-fabric roof is designed as a piece of composite engineering in which the stressed fabric membrane works with its supporting steel arches, reducing the number of steel members.

The design is more akin to that of an umbrella than a building. It is naturally-ventilated – a hollow concrete floor houses heating and draws in cool air which is discharged via vents in the roof.

JURY COMMENT The New Foyer Gallery does a number of simple things very well indeed. The architects have skilfully graded the gravelled forecourt so that it runs seamlessly into the entrance ramp, reinforcing the sense of arrival and conducting the visitor effortlessly into the complex. The building merges with the garden in which it is set and there are sculptures both inside and out. Indeed the building itself is a beautiful object both in the daytime and at night, when the fabric roof glows.

ADDRESS Falkner Road, Farnham, Surrey
CLIENT The Surrey Institute of Art and Design, University College
CONTRACTOR Mansell plc
STRUCTURE Buro Happold
CONTRACT VALUE £425,000

Snell Associates

New Foyer Gallery

Arts and leisure

Snell Associates

Sheep Field Barn Gallery

This new gallery fills a gap in the facilities at the Henry Moore Foundation, providing a space to house medium-sized sculptures and drawings. They have created a simple gallery out of an existing barn. In fact it was a steel-frame, asbestos-clad shed ordered by Moore himself towards the end of his life, which was used partly as a store for packing cases and moulds, partly for winter shelter for a tenant farmer's sheep – hence the name. Although the frame needed to be strengthened, its reuse bypassed green-belt planning restrictions. The cladding has been replaced with blackened timber in the local vernacular and the roof with standing seam zinc panels. A mechanical ventilation system is used in the display and circulation areas, with micro-climates created within the picture frames of works on paper, obviating the need for air conditioning.

JURY COMMENT Henry Moore was a thrifty Yorkshireman and all the buildings done in his time are studies in economy of means. Producing new work, while maintaining the general atmosphere of the estate, presents problems. Moore would not have liked a building with any 'show' or that made an undue fuss about the display of his sculpture. The merit of this building is in the restraint the architects have shown in conforming with Moore's own views. It is well built with reasonable quality materials and will accurately give the illusion of being something Moore might have created himself.

ADDRESS Much Hadham, Herts
CLIENT The Henry Moore Foundation
CONTRACTOR John Mowlem & Co plc
STRUCTURE Price & Myers
CONTRACT VALUE £488,000

Hawkins\Brown

Sheep Barn Gallery

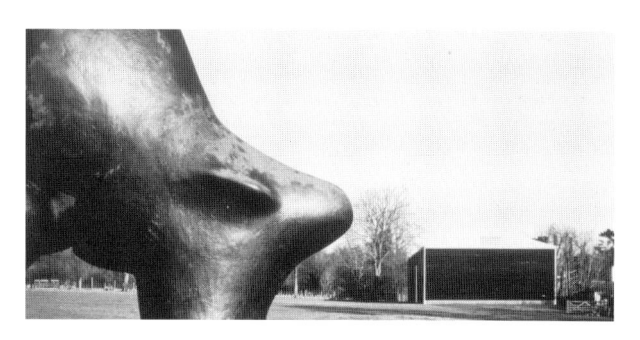

Arts and leisure

Hawkins\Brown

Tricycle Cinema

The 300-seat cinema, together with theatre rehearsal studio, offices, bar and art gallery on Kilburn High Road, represents the third and final stage of development of the Tricycle and completes Tim Foster's two decades of involvement. The foyer is a top-lit, double-height space that draws the audience into the rest of the building. The cinema, dug 4.5 metres into the ground to minimise its impact on a residential street, is approached via limestone steps, and the use of colour counteracts the basement feel. Above is a steel and glass structure containing the studios, topped with an asymmetrical butterfly roof to maximise daylight.

JURY COMMENT This is the best cinema any of us has visited. Great emphasis has been placed on the comfort of the user. The auditorium is elegant, spacious and colourful and all the details have been thoroughly controlled by the architect, a welcome change from most cinemas. The client, artistic director Nicholas Kent, has been involved in the physical development of the Tricycle for 15 years. He has set out to achieve a building of the highest quality and fought for it relentlessly. Though largely funded by the Arts Council Lottery Fund, significant funding was raised privately. That and the way the whole arts complex has been developed as and when funds have become available, makes the whole thing very human and the complete antithesis of the get-rich-quick lottery scheme.

ADDRESS Tricycle Theatre, Kilburn High Road, London NW6
CLIENT Tricycle Theatre Co Ltd
CONTRACTOR Grist Construction
STRUCTURE Price & Myers
CONTRACT VALUE £1.7 million

Tim Foster Architects

Tricycle Cinema 71

Arts and leisure

Tim Foster Architects

Colinton Parish Church New Rooms

The architects have inserted a large modern building into the burial ground of an elegant Edwardian church by Sidney Mitchell. The wider context is provided by a manse whose garden inspired Robert Louis Stevenson to write *A Child's Garden of Verses* and by a wooded valley. The new buildings seem to fit precisely because they have avoided pastiche and used materials confidently in a rigorous design. Meetings were held with the local planning department and with Historic Scotland; as a result this scheme was chosen instead of ad hoc additions to existing rooms.

The new rooms provide a range of flexible spaces which can facilitate all the diverse activities of the church on one integrated site. A simple steel frame, natural stone ground-floor walls and timber-and-glass panelling to the upper storey, together with a monopitch lead roof, all contribute to the impression that the building is floating above the trees. The fully-glazed foyer is the functional heart of the building, designed to draw visitors in and to connect the sanctuary, upper room, kitchen, vestry, cloakrooms and disabled toilet. The link between the foyer and sanctuary is sensitively incorporated into the existing panelled screen.

JURY COMMENT The building is a testament to the courage of both client and planners in accepting a contemporary design and to the skill of the architects in demonstrating that modern architecture can make a positive contribution to even the most sensitive site.

ADDRESS Dell Road, Edinburgh
CLIENT Colinton Parish Church
CONTRACTOR JB Bennett Ltd, Glasgow
STRUCTURE Oscar Faber
CONTRACT VALUE £523,000

Page and Park

Colinton Parish Church New Rooms 73

Civic and community

Page and Park

Fife Christian Counselling Centre

The single-storey building had been empty for fifteen years when taken over by the trust. The architect – who like all the professionals and craftsmen gave his time free – proposed demolishing part of the rear of the building, which had filled the site, to create a yard, helping to breathe light into a windowless corner of the building. Internal partitions were used to create counselling rooms and an inner sanctuary. Double doors were made for privacy, the outer one being transparent, the inner solid. Throughout, the techniques and materials (also given free) were chosen for ease of use by volunteers. Even so, it took five years to complete the project, which provides a free service for anyone who cannot afford to pay for counselling.

JURY COMMENT The reality is the best possible example of the difference between architecture and building. The fact that it was built over an extended period for absolutely nothing by volunteers, only enhances the achievement. We were spell-bound by the interior, with words such a stunning, breathtaking and spiritual being used in our discussions. The use of colour is astonishing – each room or space is painted a different and vibrant colour. If ever a project was needed to demonstrate the power and potential of architecture, this is it. Both the architects and the lay assessor felt that it had redefined for them their understanding of architecture. Literally, it has to be seen to be believed.

ADDRESS High Street, Leslie, Fife
CLIENT Trustees, Fife Christian Counselling Centre
CONTRACTOR all work donated
CONTRACT VALUE nil (costed at £92,000)

James Bryson

Fife Christian Counselling Centre 75

Civic and community

James Bryson

Fourth Church of Christ, Scientist

The architects have created a compact church on the two lower floors of a Portland-stone clad commercial building dating from the 1950s. The move from premises across the street was intended to give the church a much higher public profile and the scheme has done that, in a suitably quiet manner. The detailing throughout reflects the air of spirituality that envelopes the church. Full-height oak doors on the chamfered corner are opened up before a service in order to welcome people into the church and so that passers-by get glimpses through a glazed screen of the foyer and bookshop. Inside, the church is cleverly planned to offer further intriguing views and volumes. The basement is opened up to create an auditorium whose volume appears to be increased with glazed screens which give views of borrow space beyond. High ground-floor ceilings have allowed for the insertion of a steel mezzanine at the back of the bookshop which creates study areas.

JURY COMMENT A hierarchy of sensitive details has been introduced which expresses the relative importance of the different parts of the building. Access to the first floor office and Sunday-School area is via a folded plate steel stair whose exposed soffit ripples down into the basement, modulating the journey from the quotidian to the sacred. We were particularly impressed by the high standard of workmanship that had been achieved and the pride with which the building is being maintained.

ADDRESS Peter Street, Manchester
CLIENT Fourth Church of Christ, Scientist
CONTRACTOR G & J Seddon Ltd, Manchester
CONTRACT VALUE £460,000

OMI Architects

Fourth Church of Christ Scientist 77

Civic and community

OMI Architects

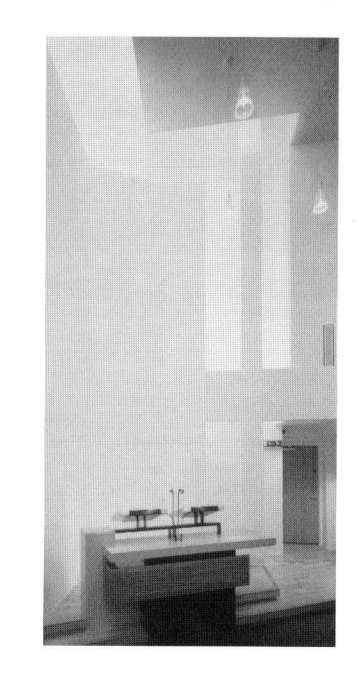

Market Lane Public Conveniences

This prosaic 1950s public toilet has been transformed into a high-quality public building which retains its original function. The scheme is part of a wider study by the architects for long-term rejuvenation of the area. The remodelled toilets have created a small square, used as a market, adding value to the area far beyond the original brief. The architects have turned the internal circulation of the building through 90 degrees, bringing it to the front and placing it behind a glazed screen. Here sits the attendant, who can monitor security and give change. The services form another opaque screen, hiding the cubicles. The surprising transparency of the front elevation encourages people to use the building: parents can wait outside and not feel they have lost all contact with their children and there are magnificent views from the inside across the square. The architects have been commissioned by the city council to design more toilets.

JURY COMMENT The design has removed the smuttiness associated with public toilets and created a building to make people smile. The toilets are within sight of the cathedral but the architects have not been afraid to design in a contemporary idiom. They have cleverly incorporated a tourist information office into the building and it now features in many tourists' holiday snaps. The design deserves to be held up as an example of creative redefinition of a building type.

ADDRESS Winchester, Hants
CLIENT Winchester City Council
CONTRACTOR Grist Construction
STRUCTURE Anthony Ward Partnership
CONTRACT VALUE £170,000

architecture plb

Market Lane Public Conveniences   **79**

Civic and community

architecture plb

The Peace Gardens

The Peace Gardens form a key part of the first phase of the Heart of the City scheme to reinvent the public realm in Sheffield, the other elements being Town Hall Square and Hallam Square. Together they replace uninspired landscaping from the 1960s and 1970s.

Set against the formality of the town hall, the Peace Gardens are an exuberant celebration of the city's regeneration. The plan is a simple circle with a fountain. Four wide paths radiate from the fountain. Raised lawns are further delineated by stone plinths, ideal for sitting on. At the end of each path is a bright ceramic cascade, with water tumbling down the steps from a pair of bronze urns. The fountain itself is meant for play. Children can squeeze between the jets without getting wet, or the more adventurous can discover that by sitting on one jet they can make the others play higher.

JURY COMMENT Every element of the design has been carefully considered and the involvement of a wide range of artists and craftsmen in the conception, design and making has added a special richness to the scheme. Stone sofas, wooden benches, metal waste bins are all detailed with consistency, boldness, humour and quality. Even the planting of the beds between the steps is a far cry from the normal regimented, uniformly-coloured municipal beds. Sheffield's Heart of the City project is an undoubted success and will be an encouragement to others to be bold and brave in regenerating their urban landscape.

ADDRESS Sheffield
CLIENT Sheffield City Council
CONTRACTOR Tilbury Douglas Construction Ltd
CONTRACT VALUE £11,280,000

Sheffield Design and Property

The Peace Gardens

Civic and community

Sheffield Design and Property

River Irthing Bridge

This footbridge reinstates a river crossing on the line of Hadrian's Wall. Previously walkers had to make a major detour across farm land. The county council held a competition to select a design for a minimum-impact bridge which would take account of the different heights of the two banks and would not cause blockage during flooding.

The Napper Partnership's winning design provides a 32-metre span with a second 8-metre cantilevered back span which obviates the need for heavy abutments. The bridge has two curved, tapered, main beams, slightly splayed, which heighten the drama of crossing from the higher wooded escarpment on the west bank to the meadows of the flood plain on the east. The main structure was prefabricated and helicoptered in, reducing the risk of damage to the site. It is made of Corten A steel which is weathering to a deep purple-brown and blends perfectly with the peat-stained waters. The deck consists of easily-replaceable timber panels.

JURY COMMENT Without unnecessary structural gymnastics this new bridge provides a crossing which combines grace with drama and practicality. The design is uncompromisingly modern but at the same time reflects the sensitivity and history of its setting. It is simple, uncomplicated, effective in its design and detailing, and has resulted from a carefully considered client brief and a close working relationship between all concerned – an exemplary project.

ADDRESS Hadrian's Wall, near Gilsland, Northumberland
CLIENT The Countryside Agency/Cumbria County Council
CONTRACTOR John Laing Construction Ltd
STRUCTURE Ove Arup & Partners
CONTRACT VALUE £160,000

The Napper Partnership

River Irthing Bridge 83

Civic and community

The Napper Partnership

Royal Victoria Dock Bridge

The Royal Victoria Dock is a spectacular oblong of water, an aquatic equivalent of the City Airport runway just to the east. The bridge, all chunky elegance, reunites the two revivified bits of London that were put asunder when the dock was created.

The promenade along the upper level of the bridge, reached by stairs or lift, gives impressive views of what little activity there is in the dock (expect the Fleet for the Millennium), Canary Wharf and the dome. The closed ends give the impression of a ship's deck floating above its surroundings. Phase 2 plans for a gondola carrying up to 40 passengers in a parabolic arc 4 metres under the bridge deck. This has been delayed pending recommencement of the development on the north side of the dock. Six conical masts are tied down by cables, with further cables carrying tension forces to the ground via distinctive bowsprits. Steel is used for all the structural elements, with perforated stainless-steel cladding on the stairs, lifts and balustrades. Handrails and decking are made of hardwood.

JURY COMMENT The height and slim proportions of the steel structure seemed so apt. The deck feels very special, in an area where places of any human scale are generally absent. We were impressed by the unusual engineering of the truss structure and the elegance of the underside of the bridge. We all agreed it was beautiful.

ADDRESS Silvertown, London E16
CLIENT RODMA
CONTRACTOR Kier London Ltd
STRUCTURE Techniker Ltd
CONTRACT VALUE £5 million

Lifschutz Davidson

Royal Victoria Dock Bridge

Lifschutz Davidson

St David's National Park Visitor Centre

The competition brief called for a building which demonstrated respect for the past, confidence in the present, and faith in the future. As well as providing a visitor centre for people arriving in St David's, the scheme includes a new car park, planted with Pembrokeshire hedgebanks, linked to the centre by a series of pedestrian routes, and creates a new public car-free space for use by street entertainers.

The form of the building reflects the idea of the stone circle: a single-storey arc incorporating information and exhibitions and a conical-roofed rotunda with toilets and meeting room. A massive stone wall defines the space; a plain, curving, zinc-clad roof hovers over it.

JURY COMMENT The main space will not be seen at its best until funds are secured for an appropriate exhibition fit-out. The use of carpets, at the baffling insistence of the Welsh Tourist Board, has prevented an overall feeling of robustness. But these misgivings are over-ridden by the high level of skill and care in the realisation of the conceptual ideas. Attention to detail has not led to a feeling of self-conscious 'design' and, given the boldness of form, the building is surprisingly at one with its setting. It seems that the client, Philip Roach, played the main role in steering what was seen by some as a radical solution through the usual array of obstacles. He is clearly passionate about this building and has a strong belief in the power of architecture to communicate to the public.

ADDRESS St David's, Pembrokeshire
CLIENT Pembrokeshire Coast National Park Authority
CONTRACTOR tpt Construction
STRUCTURE Thorburn Colquhoun
CONTRACT VALUE £750,000

Smith Roberts Associates

St David's National Park Visitor Centre 87

Civic and community

Smith Roberts Associates

Southwark Gateway

The borough chose, with the Architecture Foundation, a number of practices to improve the streets around Bankside and Borough. This scheme improves access, orientation and safety by London Bridge. The area was inconsistently and poorly surfaced, traffic railings severed pedestrian connections and a lack of signs resulted in a desolate, disorienting gateway to the borough. The result, after 24-hour filming of the area's public use, followed by extensive consultation, addresses these problems and includes two landmarks: a dramatic angled Portland stone needle 16 metres long and a tourist information office, inserted under a concrete walkway. Here a curved glass window acts as projection screen and as a source of light at night, helping to make safe a once forbidding area.

JURY COMMENT Maximum effect with limited means has been achieved throughout the whole project with highly strategic interventions commissioned from a variety of young designers. Eric Parry's three-dimensional arrangement of the sloping pavements and the needle make an enjoyable ensemble, as well as reminding the pedestrian approaching the bridge that the natural ground level is far below. Unusually for something so small, the project achieves a complex and enigmatic character, appearing very differently from its different approach points. This small project impressed with its ingenuity, realising a complex ambition out of a difficult and unpromising situation.

ADDRESS Tooley Street, London SE1
CLIENT London Borough of Southwark
CONTRACTOR Mansell
STRUCTURE Adams Kara Taylor
CONTRACT VALUE £650,000

Eric Parry Architects

Southwark Gateway 89

Civic and community

Eric Parry Architects

Valencia Congress Centre

The centre serves as a focal point in an area of new urban development in this historic Mediterranean city. It also provides three main auditoria for around 2200 people, nine seminar rooms, as well as administrative offices, exhibition and retail areas. The building draws its inspiration from the light and shade of the city – this is no collection of black boxes. The transparent enclosure defines this relationship, drawing in light, filtering and sculpting it. Visitors approach across bridges over water which laps against the 200-metre eastern façade of the building. This water is used to cool air to ventilate the foyer. Reflected sunlight, balanced by a translucent *brise-soleil* also naturally illumines the foyer. The sweeping zinc-coated aluminium roof, has, like many in the region, two layers. The lower is a concrete shell; a gap between the two increases insulation. Local skills, techniques and materials are combined throughout with the minimum of imported components and systems.

JURY COMMENT Often conference centres tend to relate inwards and are somewhat claustrophobic and ill-mannered towards adjacent townscape. This is not the case in Valencia. Despite the high quality of the interior and the auditoria in particular, the Foster building is outward-looking and from the exterior manages to be both translucent and transparent. Even on a dull day, the principal impression is of lightness. Many people we spoke to were proud that their city had commissioned Norman Foster.

ADDRESS Avenida de las Cortes Valencianas, Valencia, Spain
CLIENT Ajuntement de Valencia
CONTRACTOR Dragados. Necso
STRUCTURE Ove Arup & Partners
CONTRACT VALUE £17 million

Foster and Partners

Valencia Congress Centre 91

Civic and community

Foster and Partners

Adam Opel Haus, Conference Centre and Campus

The brief was to create a new campus identity for the company which dominates this small central German town. This was achieved by designing two new buildings - one a headquarters, the other a conference centre, and integrating them with the existing buildings by upgrading entrances and introducing solar controlled façades, as well as by creating piazzas, gardens, lakes, roads and covered walkways. The scheme provides office space for 1300, conference facilities and a restaurant for 5500 who work in the immediate vicinity. More ambitious still was the aim to create a new concept of industrial tourism, with a factory tour, interactive exhibition, outdoor arena and dark ride.

JURY COMMENT What impresses most is the sheer scale of the project. To co-ordinate the large team involved in a scheme of this size – particularly given the inevitable complications of running such a job abroad – is a considerable achievement. To produce such consistent quality is still more remarkable. The whole thing is a masterpiece of site organisation. Much of what has been done is familiar but it has been executed with care, imagination and flair. The campus is of a standard to which all commercial buildings should aspire. Commercial firms like BDP are now routinely doing work that would once have been considered exceptional in the field. The stakes have been raised and that is good news for us all.

ADDRESS Ruby Ring, Rüsselsheim, Germany
CLIENT Adam Opel AG
CONTRACTOR Philipp Holzmann AG – Frankfurt, headquarters; Bilfinger + Berger – Wiesbaden, conference centre
STRUCTURE BDP
CONTRACT VALUE £92 million

Building Design Partnership

Adam Opel Haus, Conference Centre and Campus 93

Commercial

Building Design Partnership

Adshel R&D Centre

Using the backland behind a line of their own 3D advertising hoardings, facing on to Cromwell Road, the company now has a design studio, R&D facility and office. The architects have achieved this by looping the access road around the building and dotting it with bus shelters, smaller hoardings, illuminated signs and other pieces of well-designed street furniture.

The rear wall of the building is solid blockwork, providing noise- as well as thermal-insulation. The front is fully glazed and supported by steel columns. It is protected from the sun by a long, tilted, cantilevered canopy made of a softly inflated foil. This self-cleaning material filters daylight and can be used as a projection screen. It has already provided a New York skyline as a backdrop for bus shelters designed for the city by Richard Meier. Internally the building is conceived as a walk-through presentation of company products, with a generous entrance foyer, large meeting room and double-height workshop, with design studios and offices on the first floor.

JURY COMMENT The whole scheme gives the visiting client the impression that they are on a Hollywood film set rather than in a showroom. Adshel chose the architects through the RIBA's Clients' Advisory Service and this scheme shows how well the service works, providing as it does a great example of successful collaboration between designer and client.

ADDRESS Philbeach Gardens, Cromwell Road, London SW5
CLIENT Adshel
CONTRACTOR Constructive Interiors, Wimbledon
STRUCTURE Atelier
CONTRACT VALUE £1.9 million

Apicella Associates (now Pentagram Designs Ltd)

Adshel R&D Centre 95

Commercial

Apicella Associates (now Pentagram Designs Ltd)

MABEG Offices

This ambitious commission – a moderate-sized German office fittings company using an international architects' firm to create its headquarters on an industrial estate – is the product of years of collaboration. The result is the office-box, described by its owners as a think-tank, a sleek silver structure clad in corrugated aluminium, on 5-metre-high concrete stilts. The window bands run almost the entire building circumference with elegant perforated metal louvres following the curves of each corner. Aircraft landing lights on both top and bottom corners warn planes and lorries, adding drama, though superfluous in the former case. Access is by a partially suspended external staircase – the steps are of the aluminium profiles used on oil-rigs – as well as by lift. This vertical element in cobalt blue anchors the two floors to the central core. A small drawbridge at the base of the stair makes it look like a just-landed space-craft.

JURY COMMENT That a small project in such an unpromising location has resulted in architecture of the highest quality is largely down to the exemplary match between client and architect. The use of the firm's own office systems for reception desk and bar providing continuity between the functions of HQ and showroom, typifies this relationship. Externally, it is a refined and excellent example of a tried-and-tested type; what really makes it stand out from the run-of-the-mill metal box on legs, is its truly imaginative and beautifully done staircase.

ADDRESS Ferdinand-Gabriel Weg, Soest, Germany
CLIENT Mabeg-Kreuschner
CONTRACTOR ten regional contractors
STRUCTURE DGP
CONTRACT VALUE DM3 million

Nicholas Grimshaw & Partners

MABEG Offices

Nicholas Grimshaw & Partners

Mersey Valley Processing Centre

Placing a structure 200-metres long by 30-metres high is a tough brief. The architects have responded to North West Water's requirement – following a ban on dumping waste at sea – for a facility to incinerate and recycle sludge from Manchester and Merseyside, by depressing the structure into the slope of the land. The 'import' treatment facilities are housed under a sweeping curved roof, while 'export' is handled in free-standing buildings around the perimeter, helping to diminish the scale. The 'plume-free' chimney provides a visual counterbalance. The wall cladding consists of flat, fine or coarsely corrugated silver metal panels contrasting with buff-coloured fairfaced blockwork. Walls are glazed at upper levels – selectively at lower level – allowing views in and out of the building and flooding it with light. Workshops and a substation use gently curved roofs to echo the form of the principal buildings, and they also share a similar palette of materials.

JURY COMMENT This building illustrates the harmony that can be achieved, to the extent that it is impossible to tell whether each part has been determined by a response to the context or to the industrial processes within. The collaboration of the client with the architects has brought a work of architecture to an industrial landscape where architecture is not a part of the tradition. The client has demonstrated a considerable pride in their contribution to this fine achievement.

ADDRESS Bennett's Lane, Widnes, Cheshire
CLIENT North West Water Ltd
CONTRACTOR Tarmac Construction, Wirral
STRUCTURE DGP
CONTRACT VALUE £12 million

Austin-Smith : Lord

Mersey Valley Processing Centre

Commercial

Austin-Smith : Lord

Motorola – General Products Division

All buildings are by definition symbolic whether their author intends it or not. It is not insignificant that the makers of the latest James Bond film chose the Motorola building as a location. From the hill into which it is cut, the long silver-grey building looks like the futurist spacecraft of one of Bond's evil enemies. The planning diagram shows an extendible spine carrying services, toilets, meeting rooms and so on, with the manufacturing and office spaces clipped on.

The site has been carefully landscaped with trees, a meadow of wild flowers and grassy mounds from soil excavated during construction. Clad in glass and silver aluminium, the company headquarters is a shining new landmark, highly visible from all major routes into the town.

JURY COMMENT This is a clever solution: for a building of its type, it is built to a very tight budget, and yet the designers have developed sophisticated details and spaces which must be a delight to work in – no mean feat in an operation which is centred around rows and rows of robotic machines, which in themselves are probably worth more than the building. The co-ordination of services and structure is apparently effortless. The overall 'ceiling effect' in the manufacturing space would be at home in a department store. Even the temporary works in anticipation of expansion have been treated with great care: the staff restaurant and particularly the toilet pods are good examples.

ADDRESS Groundwell, Blunsden, Swindon, Wiltshire
CLIENT Motorola Ltd
CONTRACTOR Tilbury Douglas Construction Ltd, Birmingham
STRUCTURE Mott MacDonald
CONTRACT VALUE £41.5 million

Sheppard Robson

Motorola – General Products Division

Commercial

Sheppard Robson

One 17 AD Architects' Offices

The architects have converted a Grade II-listed stable block and bell tower in the grounds of the local rugby club, into their own offices. They share the space with a radio station, a quantity surveyor and a business consultancy. The aim throughout has been to blend contemporary design with the building's traditional features, resulting in simple, powerful detailing. A double-height entrance lobby opens on to a reception area and a meeting room. Changes in level define the functions of the spaces on the ground floor. On the first floor are offices, with directors' offices on one side of the central hall and design offices on the other. The original roof trusses have been kept and new walls and screens inserted with minimum impact. French windows at the rear provide light, natural ventilation and help create a pleasant working atmosphere.

JURY COMMENT The architects have achieved a simple but stylish design where the new works in synergy with the old and which has been completed with remarkable economy. Despite the low budget, it gives the feel and appearance of quality by the careful and sensitive manipulation of materials and internal space. It is rich in commodity and delight – the benchmark of good architecture. For potential clients of the practice which designed and uses the building, it will illustrate the significant benefits of quality and value for money that can be achieved if one pays one's architect just a little bit more than the bare minimum.

ADDRESS Brewery Drive, Huddersfield
CLIENT Huddersfield Rugby Union Football Club
CONTRACTOR J Lee Roofing
STRUCTURE Robinson Associates
CONTRACT VALUE £140,000

One 17 AD

One 17 AD Architects Offices

One 17 AD

Operational Facilities for Orange Personal Communication Services

This elegant box strikes a classical note in an undistinguished campus. Orange wanted their new call centre to unify the wider site. The principles of feng shui were used in the site design and the building itself.

A single glazed wall (60 metres long by 9 metres high) illumines the building by day with solar shades and blinds to reduce glare. It is etched with signage and lit by night to emphasise the company's ethos of approachability. Large open-plan areas house the call-centre operations on either side of the central core. Circulation is defined by single-storey pods providing lockers, reprographics and conference rooms. 'Service trees' or columns, either side of the core, support oval diffusers that affect the light from circular rooflights like leaves of a tree filtering sunlight.

The building provides a democratic working environment, and the high standard of welfare provision helps relieve the tedium of much of the work. Great emphasis is placed on the internal environment overall. Natural resources such as light and fresh air are efficiently harnessed to produce a controlled, comfortable and effective working environment. The building was opened by Prime Minister Tony Blair in June 1998.

JURY COMMENT Overall the design quality and competence, the clarity of thought and the client's consistency of philosophy and approach, which underscore this building, provide inspiration to those who struggle with the meanness and short-sightedness of most commercial development.

ADDRESS Lingfield Way, Darlington, Co. Durham
CLIENT Orange Plc
CONTRACTOR Taylor Woodrow Construction (Northern)
STRUCTURE WSP
CONTRACT VALUE £7.5 million

Nicholas Grimshaw & Partners Ltd

Operational Facilities for Orange Personal Communication Services

Nicholas Grimshaw & Partners Ltd

Photonics Centre

The architects were invited to enter a competition to design this complex of buildings, including laboratories, workshops, offices and a production hall, with facilities for optics research and laser technology. They produced a pair of sinuous buildings whose contours measured up to the clients' requirements. Units to let are laid out at right angles to the main spine, with services distributed via U-shaped concrete beams. The glass façade needs solar shading, provided by coloured venetian blinds which require careful management but allow for individual control.

JURY COMMENT The use of the buildings for optical laboratories has cleverly given rise to one of its more interesting features: the use of colour on the perimeter columns and blinds. A novel spectral colour scheme in 36 different shades was developed to give the impression that the building is clad in colour and to enhance the oscillatory appearance of the wave like façade. This concept gives the building its unique appearance. It also produces some beautiful internal spaces which are surprisingly calm given the vibrant nature of the colour scheme – and the processes that go on inside. Most striking of all is the main workshop area, empty on our visit, which in scale and the bold use of colour is almost cathedral-like. The overall result is an arresting design which clearly demonstrates that, even when confronted with a commercial brief, there is always the opportunity to create designs of merit.

ADDRESS Rudower Chaussée, Berlin, Germany
CLIENT Wista Management GmbH
CONTRACTOR C Baresel
STRUCTURE Krebb & Kiefer
CONTRACT VALUE £18.2 million

sauerbruch hutton architects

Photonics Centre 107

Commercial

sauerbruch hutton architects

Rare Ltd, New Headquarters

The clients, who are highly successful developers of computer games, were concerned that their new headquarters should be 'noticed but not noticeable'. Extensive discussions took place with the local planning authorities, with the Royal Fine Art Commission, and with the public. A masterplan produced a solution of buildings that are largely traditional and closed on the entrance side and more open and unconventional on the other. The workspaces, or 'barns', are linked with glazed corridors. The landscaping, including lakes that will treat surface water and sewage, is essential to the overall plan, and this will be implemented over time. The 'barns' are clad in cedar, while one main elevation of the administration block is clad in prepatinated copper, the other in brick. The buildings are naturally ventilated and use a building management system to control night cooling.

JURY COMMENT The low-energy design of the building has determined much of its form, but they are by no means rhetorical, rather entirely practical. There is an emphasis on comfort, with casual and incidental uses revealing the attention to the well-being of a workforce that has to work late. The materials and their colours play down the fact that this is a high specification building in a lovely rural setting. It is detailed with restraint and control throughout. We enjoyed this visit and found it to be better than anticipated. There was a buzz of excitement among all the staff we met and there is a very good match between the client and the architects.

ADDRESS Atherstone
CLIENT Rare Ltd
CONTRACTOR Wates Construction
CONTRACT VALUE £6 million

Feilden Clegg Architects

Rare Ltd, New Headquarters

Feilden Clegg Architects

Thorp Architectural Modelmakers

Thorp Modelmakers wanted a building which would advertise their services and would make a clear statement about their interest in materials and the ways in which they can be assembled. The result is a striking contemporary building, in a conservation area, that is environmentally friendly to its neighbours. Their response places a residential frontage to the main street, with vehicle access to the model-making studio and conference centre from the rear. The asymmetrical curved roof bridges the gap between the domestic scale of the houses and the more formal elevation of the business premises. The project cleverly addresses environmental concerns. The need for air conditioning in the main studio is avoided by an overhang at eaves level and by the use of motorised external blinds and grey anti-sun glass. Large sliding doors provide ventilation in summer. Noise is dealt with by placing machinery in sound attenuated rooms. Dust is collected and treated before being silently discharged.

JURY COMMENT We were particularly impressed by the inventive detailing in the main elevation. While careful thought has been given to contextual design when it comes to existing buildings, some new houses by the modelmakers themselves – with belated and reluctant input from the architects – have somewhat spoilt the effect. It is regrettable that the same quality of design exemplified by the studios and workshop has not been carried through into the residential development.

ADDRESS Whitmore Lane, Sunningdale, Berkshire
CLIENT Nick and Neville Mines
CONTRACTOR Barnes & Elliott
STRUCTURE Anthony Hunt Associates
CONTRACT VALUE £467,000

Corrigan + Soundy + Kilaiditi Architects

Corrigan + Soundy + Kilaiditi Architects

Commercial

Waterside, British Airways

This scheme places the concept of the street firmly in the public realm. Waterside was planned as a catalyst to transform the way British Airways runs its business. By placing all its administrative functions in one complex, the company has used the latest ideas in space planning, office technology and management thinking to change its business culture. But the overall plan, designed by Norwegian Niels Torp and delivered by Renton Howard Wood Levin, of a 175-metre main street, complete with landscaping and stream, used for social activities including shopping, with neighbourhoods of six four-storey 'houses' of open-plan offices, was also influenced by its remoteness from any urban centre. Outside the 40-acre site, BA were obliged, as part of the planning-gain agreement, to de-contaminate and landscape as a public park a further 240 acres. Harmondsworth now has a public space the size of Kensington Gardens.

JURY COMMENT The building remains a great example of how a large company, through being open-minded, can benefit from an innovative design team. Indeed the radical reinvention of the workplace is perhaps the building's greatest achievement.

Other judges however found the building, 'heavy handed, not least in the unimaginative, repetitious open-plan offices.'

ADDRESS Harmondsworth, Middlesex
CLIENT British Airways
CONTRACTOR Mace Ltd
STRUCTURE Buro Happold
CONTRACT VALUE £200 million

Niels Torp / RHWL Partnership

Waterside, British Airways 113

Commercial

Niels Torp / RHWL Partnership

All Saints Church

The brief called for new elements to be added to a church that had become so neglected and dilapidated that it had been the subject of a number of Dangerous Structures Notices. Today the once neglected church has become – in the best medieval tradition – the centre of the local community: a busy place of worship, an extension of the street, a short-cut through the town, with facilities including a meeting place, a vegetarian café and a public lavatory.

The project ethos can be summed up as: if it ain't bust, don't fix it; replacement should be on a like-for-like basis; and any intervention should be of its age. Each new element is designed to be independent of the fabric of the church, with the necessary technology for its purpose plumbed in. The prefabricated 'pods' can moved or removed without damaging the historic church, which retains its power and sense of place. The first pod is a new vestry, where the need for privacy and dignity is matched by regard for safety and elegance; the second a high-specification kitchen for the café; and the third is the trio of unisex lavatories, with the parish office above. The work was partially funded by English Heritage and the Heritage Lottery Fund.

JURY COMMENT In all cases the interventions are successful and the café provides a small regular income to the church. In the photographs the built elements look curious and heavy, possibly over-detailed, but when seen in the space, the scale and detailing is appropriate.

ADDRESS High Street, Hereford
CLIENT All Saints Church PCC
CONTRACTOR C Honey (Builders) Ltd, Hereford
CONTRACT VALUE £700,000

Rod Robinson Associates

All Saints Church 115

Rod Robinson Associates

Trinity College, Lecture Room Block

The brief called for new social facilities for students to be created out of a lecture theatre dating from the 1830s. The ground floor provides three different bar areas: for real-ale drinkers, for the white-wine-and-Perrier set, and for those who prefer coffee. The architects have used a range of natural materials and there is a delicate sense of asymmetrical composition. The first floor has separate reading rooms for graduates and undergrads. Here the architects have reinstated the integrity of the building with double-height windows at either end. On the second floor, acoustic boxes seal in the noise from television rooms, while within the undergrad TV room, sliding screens allow for flexibility when major TV events clash.

JURY COMMENT This is an example of uncompromising, good modern design set in the context of imaginative conservation work on a good-quality historic building. The new work has produced a set of fine stylish and evidently modern interiors. The shell into which the conversion is set has been restored to give back important double-order windows that had been lost in earlier conversions. The most engaging aspect is a symmetrical double staircase either side of a window, through which each flight can be seen as a mirror image of the other. This is a memorable space and suggests a high order of architectural imagination. One often doesn't notice at first what has been achieved by a project but the combination of levels and windows has produced new and unexpected views of the Cambridge roofline.

ADDRESS Trinity College, Cambridge
CLIENT Trinity College, Cambridge
CONTRACTOR Rattee & Kett
CONTRACT VALUE £900,000

Ian Simpson Architects

Trinity College, Lecture Room Block 117

Conservation

Ian Simpson Architects

Beetham House, Riverside School

The project provides a new home for 14 young people with behavioural difficulties. In line with a very detailed brief, the architects have produced an economic building that is also generous to its occupants. The site is a former Second World War prisoners-of-war camp, but the setting is pleasant and rural, surrounded by hills on the edge of the Lake District. This is part of an overall concept by the same architects for future houses around a 'village green'. The domestic air is enhanced by the rectangular plan and simple pitched roof. The principle form of the house is simple and direct and derives as much from the commonplace buildings around it as from the modesty of the budget. A large opening, running the full width of the building in the gable end, creates a generous porch. Through this porch a series of interconnecting living, kitchen and dining spaces can be seen. A yellow-green colour scheme contrasts with the rough grey render. All the finishes are appropriately rugged yet easy to repair. Bedroom furniture is modular, of varnished glued-and-screwed plywood.

JURY COMMENT The highest possible accolade for this building comes from a report by the client that indicates that the balance struck between the homely and the functional has made the residents of this house less disruptive than those of others: a clear indicator of good architecture having a beneficial effect on social behaviour.

ADDRESS Whassett, Cumbria
CLIENT Riverside Childcare Services Ltd
CONTRACTOR Cox & Allen (Kendal) Ltd
STRUCUTRE R T James & Partners
CONTRACT VALUE £215,000

Houlton Taylor Architects

Beetham House, Riverside School 119

Education

Houlton Taylor Architects

Faculty of Management, Robert Gordon University

Foster's were commissioned to create a master plan for a new campus for the university on a greenfield site on the banks of the Dee. This first building responds to the dramatic sweeping landscape, its concrete frame terracing down a hillside. It is oversailed by a curved aluminium roof supported on narrow steel columns. Local granite alternates with aluminium in the cladding. 'Streets' make the building, with a four-storey atrium at its heart, easy to understand. Library, teaching and office areas are located off the main street. Student common rooms overlook a winter garden which opens out on to shaded river terraces.

Low-energy solutions are embodied into the design. A building-management system automatically opens and closes windows and rooflights in perimeter areas such as library, teaching and offices; internal rooms such as lecture theatres, IT rooms and the TV studio have a supplementary mechanical ventilation system. CAD was used to test the building's energy efficiency and thermal-comfort performance.

JURY COMMENT Natural local materials are used inside and out. The whole building has an order and rhythm which, with the natural colours, allow the noise and bustle of a busy university faculty to happen in a relaxed way without becoming chaotic. Physically this is helped by good acoustics. The curved roof sweeping over the whole building ties it to its site and with one bold line makes it an award-winning project.

ADDRESS Robert Gordon University, Garthdee Road, Aberdeen
CLIENT Robert Gordon University, Aberdeen
CONTRACTOR Bovis Construction Ltd
STRUCTURE Ove Arup & Partners
CONTRACT VALUE £12.8 million

Foster and Partners

Faculty of Management, Robert Gordon University

Education

Foster and Partners

International Building, Royal Holloway

Royal Holloway has a long history of commissioning distinguished buildings. The brief sought a flagship building, housing language departments, to provide an architectural riposte to the Grade I-listed Founders Building, but on a low budget. The International Building, three storey and U-shaped, turns its back on the main road. The natural slope has been used to minimise visual impact by digging the building into the ground and putting the entrance at first-floor level. Its rear elevation matches the red brick common to most of the site; the front is of cedar-clad boarding. The roof is finished in an aluminium standing-seam system.

The building is planned with a central circulation spine with teaching rooms situated off it. Social areas are close to the double-height entrance space. High-energy efficiency is achieved through a building-management system, allowing cooling by admitting night air into the hollow concrete floors via automatically opening vents.

JURY COMMENT Detailing is pleasing and consistent throughout and great care and ingenuity have been taken, as one would expect from an architectural practice whose name stands for Energy Conscious Design, to make a building which uses as little energy as possible, in terms of both embodied energy and energy in use. The result, with its façade modulated by very simple sliding louvred sun screens, is a building that is fresh and comfortable to work in – a model for higher education.

ADDRESS Egham, Surrey
CLIENT Royal Holloway, University of London
CONTRACTOR Mowlem
STRUCTURE RMJM
CONTRACT VALUE £2.8 million

ECD Architects

International Building, Royal Holloway 123

Education

ECD Architects

ISMA Centre

This building breaks new ground in the way it bridges the worlds of education and the workplace. Students are training for work in the financial sector and are provided here with simulated dealing rooms. In addition there are workstations for administration staff and PhD students, glass partitioned offices for training, a large lecture theatre and a double-height central communal café and lounge area. A glazed lift links with the open-plan first floor. The acoustics have been well handled to allow for socialising and formal and informal study to be carried on simultaneously and without distraction. Elegant furniture has been chosen in consultation with the client and reflects the ethos of the building.

Throughout the architects have taken a responsible attitude to environmental design, with as many of the spaces as possible being naturally ventilated. Outside, the building is coolly elegant and is fully glazed at its north and south ends. A curved block to the west of the central space houses seminar rooms and the professor's offices. A pitched roof mimics the gentle slope of the site.

JURY COMMENT *The internal spaces lift the spirits. The restrained use of timber against white walls and the integration of natural and artificial lighting are both particularly effective. Professor Brian Scott-Quinn was clearly a truly committed client, committed both to good modern architecture and to his own sense of adventure.*

ADDRESS Whiteknights, Reading, Berkshire
CLIENT ISMA Centre
CONTRACTOR James Longley & Co Ltd
STRUCTURE Dewhurst McFarlane & Partners
CONTRACT VALUE £1.8 million

Rick Mather Architects

ISMA Centre 125

Education

Rick Mather Architects

The Ruskin Library

The Ruskin Library provides improved conservation and access for the world's largest collection of works relating to the Victorian writer, made possible by a grant from the Heritage Lottery Fund. This jewel box of a building is rich with references to Venice and, short of writing Ruskin's name on the outside, goes as far as possible to proclaim its purpose. The building stands in a grass lagoon, approached by a bridge-like causeway. The concrete blocks sparkle with a white aggregate and contrast with bands of dark-green polished precast concrete. The stainless-steel bosses recall the fastenings used to link the marble cladding of Venetian churches. A skirt of glass allows views of the archive as it plunges into the basement. This isolation of the archive meets strict environmental requirements obviating the need for air conditioning.

Inside is a series of intimate spaces: offices, reading room and viewing galleries, which reflect Ruskin's belief in the importance of craft. This extends beyond the finishes, to the oak, walnut and leather furniture.

JURY COMMENT This building exhibits innovation in its form, the fruits of collaboration with artists and craftsmen and an imaginative exploration of materials, from the slate and glass floor at the entrance, to the oiled, rendered finish of the internal circulation walls. If there is a fault to be found it is, perhaps, that the richness of invention may rival the quality of some of the works which it is intended to exhibit.

ADDRESS Bailrigg, Lancaster
CLIENT University of Lancaster
CONTRACTOR John Laing Construction, North West Region
STRUCTURE Harris & Sutherland
CONTRACT VALUE £1.8 million

MacCormac Jamieson Prichard

The Ruskin Library

Education

MacCormac Jamieson Prichard

St Aloysius' Primary School

Somewhere there must exist a rule that insists that junior schools should be single storey, replace as many green fields as possible and cause vast quantities of fossil fuel to be burned in ferrying children to and from them. This one throws the rulebook out of one of its fifth-storey windows. It is as urban as the tenement block it replaces and as elegant as the nearby Mackintosh School of Art. It takes its place alongside the other college buildings and provides an inspiring school for 400 children. Inside, a three-storey atrium brings light into the classrooms grouped around it and forms a buzzing hub for the school. The importance and accessibility of the computer room is highlighted by its occupancy of a glass box that juts into the space.

JURY COMMENT This is a thoroughly grown-up building using predominantly glass and concrete and the main public entrance has all the feel of an expensive apartment block. Nonetheless, the children have clearly responded positively to their unusual surroundings and elements of the building have appeared unsolicited in their schoolwork. The enthusiasm and determination of the clients in this project appear to have been crucial. Father Porter's desire to contribute to the architectural vocabulary of the city and his willingness to put in long hours must have made the architects' job a great deal easier and made a significant contribution to the success of the project.

ADDRESS Hill Street, Garnethill, Glasgow
CLIENT St Aloysius' College
CONTRACTOR Lilley Construction
STRUCTURE Sidey Associates
CONTRACT VALUE £2.3 million

Elder and Cannon Architects

St Aloysius' Primary School

Elder and Cannon Architects

Shackleton Memorial Library

An entrance linking Sir Herbert Baker's original 1930s Founders Building with one from the 1960s, was demolished to create a circular structure that mediates between the rectilinear forms of the two older buildings. The new drum provides a contrasting open day-lit space which is a reference point for the site. A new storey has been added to the earlier building, constructed of lightweight panels. All elements are served by a freestanding lift in a glass shaft, inserted within the main stairwell. Cladding is in stock bricks to match the Founders Building. Windows are powder coated metal, with west-facing windows fitted with external sunscreens.

JURY COMMENT This is a well-mannered and well-constructed building that adds significantly to the collection of spaces making up the Scott Polar Research Institute. The existing building consisted of a number of densely packed floors with lots of separate spaces: the new rotunda makes sense of all this. Various nicely handled touches have been added to the building in the form of ceiling-lighting systems and areas of display. The most memorable visual idea in the interior is the glass lift, at the opposite end of the entrance lobby to the original shrine to polar exploration. It has the appearance of a shaft of ice that has plunged through the building. The colour of the glass surround and the daylight glowing through it deliberately evokes the painting of ice hung opposite to it.

ADDRESS Scott Polar Research Institute, University of Cambridge, Lensfield Road, Cambridge
CLIENT Estates Management Building Service, University of Cambridge
CONTRACTOR Haymills Ltd, Stowmarket
STRUCTURE Campbell Reith Hill
CONTRACT VALUE £1,036,689

John Miller + Partners

Shackleton Memorial Library 131

Education

John Miller + Partners

Sir Alexander Fleming Building

This may be a one-gag building– the atrium is hardly the most original of ideas but it's still a good one, and seldom has the device been handled so brilliantly and to such effect. The atrium slices through five floors, but though physically taking the core out of the building, it is what gives the Sir Alexander Fleming Building its heart. It produces a new working environment for biological and medical research, providing study, office and social areas and linking the backstage laboratory areas, which are designed to adapt to the latest requirements of research – which they did even during construction.

The size of the space counters the cramped site, bringing daylight through the sculpted 'light-wave' rooflights, into the furthest recesses. The northern elevation is of Portland stone and glass, and a glazed service tower projects and completes the corner of the Queen's Lawn. It is remarkable that a project of evident quality came in at 10 per cent less – at £1860 per square metre – than comparable education buildings.

JURY COMMENT The art installation by the Danish artist Per Arnoldi forms a dramatic backdrop to the atrium with its blend of strong colours. Indeed colour is greatly evident within the rest of the building and helps to compliment the clean detailing of all the major elements. When many universities are rejecting conventional procurement routes, this offers a great model to all educational institutes of the benefits of good design.

ADDRESS Imperial College Road, London SW7
CLIENT Imperial College
CONTRACTOR Schal International
STRUCTURE Waterman Partnership
CONTRACT VALUE £42 million

Foster and Partners

Sir Alexander Fleming Building 133

Education

Foster and Partners

Student Common Room, Grimsby College

The project involved the improvement of recreational facilities – providing bar, games, concert, events, dining and coffee bar areas – for growing student numbers on this uninspired campus of 1960s and 1970s buildings. After stripping out partitions, a space was created on the ground floor of the main teaching and administration block and expanded with a timber-framed glazed extension overlooking a courtyard, which creates an airy inside-outside space.

The rationale behind the internal arrangement was to place strategically a series of significant built objects or pieces of furniture to create both open and intimate spaces. The bar is a robust drum which unfolds when open, providing bench seating; a wooden box houses vending machines and two box-like screens with holes punched through line up with circular windows. The easily-demountable furniture has a Buckminster-Fuller feel to it. The 1960s concrete coffered ceiling has been exposed and services are suspended from it. The floor is reclaimed pitch pine, raised floor areas are reached by ramps, defined by plinths which act as seats.

JURY COMMENT This is an exemplary project and demonstrates that good design is not dependent on a substantial budget but on the creativity of the architect, the engagement of the client and the enthusiasm and commitment of all concerned. The students of Grimsby College clearly enjoy the fruits of this collaboration – lucky devils.'

ADDRESS Nuns Corner, Grimsby, Lincolnshire
CLIENT Grimsby College
CONTRACTOR sub-contractors via Estates Department
CONTRACT VALUE £150,000

Hodson Design

Student Common Room, Grimsby College 135

Education

Hodson Design

Summerfields Nursery and Education Centre

The clients needed a functional box to accommodate facilities for babies and toddlers, a 'theatre', staff areas, kitchens, outside terraces and play areas. This has been addressed by the architects in a series of paired accommodation modules, linked together with a path defined by a terracotta-coloured wall, an idea that also adds an appropriately subtle sense of order to the plan. In this way the architects have avoided both a sense of repetition and an institutional feel. The 'homebases' all have partially glazed screens and coloured sliding doors. A similar strip of colour carries on inside and defines the circulation route. A central courtyard provides flexible outdoor-play space, and a visual focus. Each unit has access directly on to a series of smaller, more intimate outdoor spaces, bounded by an elegantly detailed, horizontally slatted screen fence. Extensive research undertaken by architect and client has resulted in functional details such as sliding doors on glazed recesses, carefully positioned sinks and no traps for little fingers. The project was completed in only 22 weeks.

JURY COMMENT Set among the all-too-typical mediocrity of sprawling shops and housing, this elegant white-rendered building with a shingle-clad monopitch roof has successfully created a context of its own. Although it has been open for a year, it is impressive how little has been adapted by the users and where retrofit has occurred, it has been integrated entirely within the spirit of the original concept.

ADDRESS Dean Row Road, Wilmslow, Cheshire
CLIENT Kids Unlimited
CONTRACTOR PE Jones Contracts (Manchester) Ltd
STRUCTURE Blackwood Structural Design
CONTRACT VALUE £620,000

Stephenson Bell

Summerfields Nursery and Education Centre

Stephenson Bell

Dublin Dental Hospital

The brief called for the retention of the terracotta façade of the existing Victorian Dental Hospital, refurbishing the building for teaching, and linking it to a new Clinical building. The architects have achieved this with a new building faced with red brick where its curved façade ties in with the old, and granite and glass cladding to the rear where it addresses the grey buildings of Trinity College. The two are linked by a full-height top-lit atrium – a spectacular sculpture gallery – containing stairs and lifts, and bridges between the buildings. The clinical areas are light and airy, free of structure, and are intended to be informal and friendly. In the practical teaching areas, miniature dental surgeries are shoehorned in. Each is wedge-shaped, allowing the trainee dentist to work at the patient's head, while saving room by tapering the space around the patient's feet.

JURY COMMENT The new bits of this were very impressive. The overall plan is ingenious because the new entrance and atrium space provides a central point for orientating movement around the new and old buildings. The quality of detailing is high and confidence-inspiring; the layout of the clinical areas is imaginative and economical. There are undoubtedly lessons here for the UK's health service, which all too often produces mediocre buildings. The client claims that the architects were, in effect, recommended to him by Prince Charles many years ago, when he criticised their plans for extending the National Gallery in London.

ADDRESS Lincoln Place, Dublin 2
CLIENT Dublin Dental Hospital Board and Trinity College, Dublin
CONTRACTOR Michael McNamara Building Contractors, Dublin
STRUCTURE Ove Arup & Partners
CONTRACT VALUE IR£8 million

Ahrends Burton & Koralek

Dublin Dental Hospital

Ahrends Burton & Koralek

North Croydon Medical Centre

The medical centre is entered from a busy shopping street through a tiny courtyard which is largely enclosed but open to the sky. This space, as well as mediating between outside and in, informs, lights and orientates the whole building. Inside is a large waiting room, with a well-designed reception desk facing the door. The uncluttered feel is achieved by housing medical records on the level above, leaving receptionists free to deal with patients. This area is double height to relate it visually and acoustically to the patient areas on the first floor. It also adds a touch of grandeur.

JURY COMMENT The first view sets the scene: it revives and enlivens the workaday scene. Similar in scale to its undistinguished neighbours, it demonstrates what architecture can do while still obeying the rules: it is neither outlandish nor expensive but has brought fresh thought to an old problem. This is a fine example of the client and his consultants working together to show how architecture can lift the ordinary.

Later judges added, 'There were a few flaws – a too-utilitarian waiting room and a poor standard of furnishing, though that is surely just a question of time and budget. Overall the jury appreciated the rightness of it all. We also noted that this was exceptional for such health care buildings and therefore the design was exemplary. There was much discussion before it was agreed that this building narrowly missed being a category award winner.'

ADDRESS London Road, Thornton Heath, Surrey
CLIENT Dr R J Trew
MAIN CONTRACTOR MBC Construction
STRUCTURE Techniker
CONTRACT VALUE £582,000

Allford Hall Monaghan Morris

North Croydon Medical Centre

Allford Hall Monaghan Morris

Rushton Medical Centre

The scheme is part of the regeneration of Hoxton, housing four existing small medical practices, designed to be flexible enough to respond to new thinking in primary health care. It was executed using private finance, by the design team appointed by the health authority. The steel-frame construction with precast concrete floors uses infill blockwork walls, faced with externally rendered insulation over a brick base. The steel roof is covered with profiled aluminium. A rich colour scheme runs throughout. The ground floor houses parking, reception, administration, and a tall top-lit waiting area – with the feel of a terrace café – leading to consulting and treatment rooms. The multi-disciplinary Hoxton Health Collective and a clinical suite are located on the first floor.

JURY COMMENT The Rushton Medical Centre is a rich and spatially complex building and achieves an amazing amount within its social and economic context. It is very popular with its users and attempts to find a contemporary, humanist architectural language which can be accepted by a local population without money or expectations. Any ambivalence on the part of the jury has arisen out of some suspicion about the playful front façade and details. If one compares it with other good buildings, the clear and rich functional arrangements more than outweigh these problems.

ADDRESS Rushton Street, Hoxton, London N1
CLIENT East London & City Health Authority/Imperial Square Developments Ltd
CONTRACTOR John Barker Construction & Imperial Square Developments (Hoxton) Ltd
STRUCTURE Whitby Bird & Partners
CONTRACT VALUE £1.25 million

Penoyre & Prasad Architects

Rushton Medical Centre 143

Health

Penoyre & Prasad Architects

Blaen Camel extension

The architect has extended a cramped two-storey stone farmhouse with a single-storey space containing a second living room, a third bedroom and study, and a utility area. The new rooms are light and airy compared with the solidity of the old house. Construction methods reflect both the family's organic farming business and the architect's interest in green building, combined with other modern materials, sourced elsewhere, including large double-glazed windows and low-energy double-glazed rooflights. The frame is of green oak from nearby woods; the plinth and garden walls are from a local quarry; and insulation is provided by the farm's sheep. Critics have spotted the influence of Mies and Frank Lloyd Wright, though Louis Kahn's Kimbell Museum was the conscious influence for a series of bays which admit strips of light and blur the boundaries between inside and out.

JURY COMMENT What has emerged is an apparently modest, pitch-roofed addition that could be read as a range of simple outbuildings. But appearances are deceptive and behind the solution lies a body of ideas that questions the tendency to believe that good architecture must be sensational architecture, and challenges the current preoccupation with style over content. It is a considered, thought-provoking piece of work that deserves wider recognition. It may not deliver an eye-catching glossy image but the Seggers find it life-enhancing, which is much more important.

ADDRESS Cilcennin, Lampeter, Wales
CLIENTS Peter Segger and Anne Evans
CONTRACTOR CLS Construction Ltd, Aberystwyth
STRUCTURE Pat Borer
CONTRACT VALUE £102,000

David Lea Architect

Blaen Camel extension 145

Houses and housing

David Lea Architect

Donnelly House Extension

A change in the brief provided an unexpected opportunity for the architect to refocus the house towards the garden. Instead of a granny extension at the back of the house, the clients decided to move the living area from the front of the house, releasing the old living room to be used for the elderly relatives. This meant the new-build was more an extension to the garden than to the house, appropriately enough, since with its wooden frame and cantilevered glazed roof, it resembles a garden pavilion. Sliding glass screens complete the seamless transition from house to garden and make the most of daylight. The exterior is clad in floating planes of cedar and mahogany, giving the whole the feel of a much larger house.

JURY COMMENT This project demonstrates how good modern architecture can transform the way a house is used, simply by adding a relatively modest rear extension. Carefully and consistently detailed, the new living space and kitchen are visually and physically connected to the garden, giving the delighted clients a finished scheme way beyond their original requirements. The cost was impressively low and the money has been carefully spent: the rich combination of timbers used internally and externally suggests a more generous budget. By concentrating on the essentials of proportion, volume and light, the architect has satisfied the client brief and changed the house from mundane to remarkable.

ADDRESS Milverton Avenue, Beardsden, Glasgow
CLIENT Paul and Dominique Donnelly
CONTRACTOR C & V Construction
STRUCTURE Woolgar Hunter
CONTRACT VALUE £35,145

Christopher Platt

Donnelly House Extension 147

Houses and housing

Christopher Platt

Farmhouse addition

The planning authority encouraged an approach which was stylistically different from the main farmhouse and the architect has seized upon this rare opportunity. The design combines old and new: a variety of ceiling heights and timber details associated with older buildings, with more recent developments in construction techniques. The new-build is single storey and clad mainly in terne-coated stainless steel, which weathers to a dull light grey. The new breakfast room connects to the old kitchen but is at a lower level, retaining views from the bedrooms and giving access directly to the garden. There is a small study and a high-ceilinged living room. Large windows to the south and west exploit free solar heating and the views over Lough Neagh. Timber shutters – vertical in the study, horizontal in the living room – provide shade and control light levels.

JURY COMMENT It was a delightful surprise to come upon this discreet yet unashamedly modern farmhouse extension, which so successfully fits the rural setting. The occupants, who are to be commended for their courage in employing a young, modernist architect, are delighted by his handling of daylight and artificial light, which is further modulated by the use of colour. The new extension resolves and clarifies the existing plan and captures spectacular distant views. This is a mature, cohesive integration of new and old, without stylistic compromise.

ADDRESS Cranfield Road, Randalstown, Antrim, Northern Ireland
CLIENT private
CONTRACTOR Alistair Caldwell Building Contractor
STRUCTURE Gault Chambers Bullen
CONTRACT VALUE £36,600

Alan Jones Architects

Farmhouse addition

Alan Jones Architects

Houses and housing

Gwithian

The project involved the conversion, extension and transformation of a 1970s bungalow. The architects have retained much of the existing house and some original features, using practicality and economy of means combined with a sense of irony, while transforming the major part of the house and its orientation. Their design makes clear reference to precedent – since one of the clients is a former chief executive of English Heritage who believes that 1970s artisans' dwellings will be considered in the same way as we now think of such buildings from the 1850s, this was important. The extensions and the garden are designed with care and the many junctions are deftly handled. Through a sequence of spaces with internal views, they have raised the floor level at the back and improved the views over Rutland Water, while the front benefits from sun-catching top lights.

The centrepiece is a cockpit kitchen around which all the social spaces revolve. A number of frescoed plaster sliding panels enable further enclosure but the effect is one of light, space and calmness. Colour is used to effect a transformation from south to north, with warm colours in the sunny rooms and watery, cool colours in the areas with lakeside views.

JURY COMMENT This shows how a modest-sized project can be beautifully designed by an architect so as to fit into its own garden and the wider landscape. It stands out from other domestic projects as consistently elegant in concept and realisation.

ADDRESS Hambleton, Rutland Water, Rutland
CLIENT Ms J Page and Mr J Orme
CONTRACTOR P Waller Ltd
STRUCTURE Steve Wickham, Price & Myers
CONTRACT VALUE £145,000

Marsh and Grochowski

Gwithian

Marsh and Grochowski

Ivy Bank House

The rebuilding of the rear extension to a nineteenth-century, flat-fronted, marled stone house was commissioned by clients who admit that they don't like modern architecture, yet they say enthusiastically that Murphy's addition has changed their lives. The imminent arrival of triplets drove this project hard. The brief called for the creation of a kitchen and playroom feeding off a reconfigured dining room without increasing the dimensions. The kitchen has become a 'console', a gently curved work area, fully glazed, overlooking the garden. These windows are on a counter-weighted pivot system and can be opened up completely so that even indoor summer cooking feels like an outdoor activity. In the nursery a window seat similarly becomes part of the garden when the windows are slid back.

JURY COMMENT The essentially simple linear kitchen and square playroom beyond are given a richness and seemingly limitless variability by layers of thoughtful and intriguing detail. The exposed steel frame with its sole point of support, the curved rough-rendered wall disappearing into a mirrored return, the frameless counter-balanced windows which open to unite the kitchen with the courtyard garden, the mirrored linear rooflight, sliding corner doors to the play room, continuous clerestorey light at eaves level and countless other sure-handed details so typical of the architect, made the visit to the building a rewarding and thought-provoking experience.

ADDRESS Main Road, Dirleton, East Lothian
CLIENT Simon and Susan Morison
CONTRACTOR Inscape Joinery
STRUCTURE David Narro Associates
CONTRACT VALUE £61,000

Richard Murphy Architects

Ivy Bank House

Richard Murphy Architects

Mellangoose

Mellangoose is built on a narrow falling site, which was once the orchard of the house next door. A self-build scheme using local sub-contractors, the cost worked out at less than £100,000, despite there being three double bedrooms and two luxurious aquamarine mosaic-tiled bathrooms. The design is modern and Californian in feel. A cluster of terracotta-coloured rooms either side of a narrow top-lit slot, spill down towards a timber deck. The double-height living space provides a bright and spacious gallery for painting. Both dining-table and work surfaces in the kitchen are made of *in-situ* polished concrete.

JURY COMMENT It is a big challenge to produce a design for a low-cost house to be constructed as a self-build project and end up with award-winning architecture. The plan and cross section are both elegant and simple. The progression of spaces, glimpses of what comes next, penetration of daylight, and clarity of organisation all make the house a special place.

Though very different from a typical speculatively-built new house, the design is inherently simple and employs no unusual techniques, so much so that the owners say they would gladly do a self-build again. It should be hoped that more people will try this route to a roof over their head as a result of this very good example of the type.

ADDRESS Trescobeas Road, Falmouth, Cornwall
CLIENT Lola and Bruce McAllister
CONTRACTOR Bruce McAllister
STRUCTURE Roy Billington Associates
CONTRACT VALUE £100,000

McAllister Architects

Mellangoose 155

Houses and housing

McAllister Architects

Skywood House

The challenge to the architect-client (the managing director of Foster's) was to create as spacious a feel as possible on a site constrained by protected trees and the rigid planning regulations that apply in the greenbelt of south Buckinghamshire. The clients wanted to create a magical glass-box house that satisfied their minimalist aesthetic but also provided practical accommodation for their family of three children, plus various pets. The long twisting drive gives and takes away views of the house as it loops round the newly-created lake and past the metal waterfall that oxygenates the lake. This is essentially a self-build project, though the term gives an entirely wrong impression.

JURY COMMENT This is a mature piece of work where the level of detailing is consistent and effortless. Its composition contains quotes from the early work of Mies but its execution is contemporary. This modern pavilion on a sensitive site will inspire future architects and patrons.

Other judges though had reservations: 'In the best minimalist architecture, formal restraint lies easily alongside functional excellence. Here, when function gets in the way, it appears to be brushed aside, for example in the non-opening bedroom windows and in the too-narrow wash basins. That said, the way in which classic modern cool has been brought to Denham is admirable.' The house generated more debate than any other before the judges decided against giving it a Category Award.

ADDRESS Denham, Middlesex
CLIENT Graham and Diane Phillips
CONTRACTOR Taylor Woodrow Management
STRUCTURE Ove Arup & Partners
CONTRACT VALUE £451,000

Graham Phillips

Skywood House

Graham Phillips

Assessors

The RIBA is extremely grateful to the assessors, who give their time freely.

THE STIRLING PRIZE JURY 1999 Marco Goldschmied, Michael Manser, Rick Mather, Amanda Baillieu, Stella McCartney

THE RIBA AWARDS GROUP 1999 Michael Manser (chairman), Robert Adam, Amanda Baillieu, Ian Davidson, Stephen Hodder, Sir Christopher Howes, Amanda Levete, David Levitt, Alicia Pivaro, Sunand Prasad

REGIONAL ASSESSORS
C chair L lay assessor R regional representative

EAST MIDLANDS
C Kate Heron
L Clive Jacobs
R Steve Major

EASTERN
C Jeremy Dixon
L Vivien Lovell
R John Cole

EUROPE
Architects:
Robert Adam
Ian Davidson
Stephen Hodder
David Levitt

Lay assessors:
Amanda Baillieu
Tony Chapman
Sir Christopher Howes

LONDON (EAST)
C Peter St John
L Beatrix Campbell
R Peter McCafferty

LONDON (WEST)
C Paul Monaghan
L Simon Silver
R Raymond Stignant

NORTH WEST
C David Morley
L Doris Saatchi
R Sue Carmichael

NORTHERN
C Niall Phillips
L Seona Reid
R Christopher Dennis

NORTHERN IRELAND
C Alistair Sunderland
L Jim Berrow
R Paddy Acheson

Assessors

SCOTLAND
- C Jonathan Manser
- L Tom Sunter
- R Alan Dunlop

SOUTH EAST
- C Joanna van Heyningen
- L Keith Price
- R Denis Owen

SOUTH WEST
- C Roger Stephenson
- L Murray Grigor
- R Stan Bolt

SOUTHERN
- C Stephanie Fischer
- L Iain Tuckett
- R Richard Jobson

WALES
- C Phillip O'Dwyer
- L Cynthia Grant
- R Richard Parnaby

WESSEX
- C Roger Stephenson
- L Murray Grigor
- R Malcolm Ness

WEST MIDLANDS
- C Kate Heron
- L Clive Jacobs
- R Dean Benbow

YORKSHIRE
- C Niall Phillips
- L Seona Reid
- R Richard Dawson

Sponsors

The RIBA is grateful to all the sponsors who make the Awards possible, in particular the *RIBA Journal*, published by the Builder Group, which has replaced the *Sunday Times* as our main sponsor, providing the money for the Stirling Prize and much of the judging process. We are also grateful for the continuing support of The Arts Council of England, for the Client of the Year; to the Goldschmied Trust, for the Stephen Lawrence Prize; and to the Department of Health, for the Health Award for Architecture in Healthcare. This year we also welcome The Crown Estate as sponsors of the Conservation Award. Once again the Ellipsis book, *Architecture 99*, is sponsored by Service Point digital reprographics and communications.

All RIBA winners receive a lead plaque which is placed on the building. The RIBA is grateful for the generous support of the Lead Sheet Association in manufacturing and presenting these plaques.

The Stephen Lawrence Trust

The Stephen Lawrence Trust is a non-sectarian, non-political and non-profit-making body that aims to provide young black people with the opportunity to reach the goal Stephen was so cruelly denied, by encouraging students to apply to study architecture in the UK, in the Caribbean and in South Africa. The Lawrence family hopes that, in this way, architecture and its study will come to reflect more closely the culturally diverse communities living in and using it. The Trust is pledged to play a role in the improvement of community relations and hopes to stage an annual keynote lecture raising the profile of developments in race relations and architecture.

To find out more about the Trust (Charity registration No. 1070860) please write c/o Arthur Timothy Associates, St John's Hall, 9 Fair Street, London SE1 2XA, or phone 020 7387 9465, fax 020 7357 8079.

Picture Credits

pages 15, 17, 65 Richard Davies; pages 19, 20, 21, 31, 33, 43, 45, 99, 115, 125 Richard Bryant/Arcaid; pages 29, 59, 139 Peter Cook; pages 37, 39 Roderick Coyne; pages 39, 41, 47, 53, 55, 91, 107, 133, 143 Dennis Gilbert/View; pages 48, 49, 89, 121 Nigel Young; page 61 Martine Hamilton-Knight; pages 57, 63, 67 Martin Charles; pages 25, 69 James Morris; page 71 Page & Park Architects; page 73 Simon Addison; page 75 Jonathan Keegan; pages 77, 109 Jonathan Moore; page 79 Tony Woodcock; page 81 The Napper Partnership; page 83 Chris Gascoigne; page 85 Charlotte Wood; page 87 Nick Jackson; pages 93, 141 Tim Soar; page 95 Werner Huthmacher; pages 97, 137 Ian Lawson; page 101 Chris Nickerson – Sphere; page 103 Tim Soar; page 105 Bitter Bredt Photographic; page 111 Christine Quick; pages 113, 151 Martine Hamilton-Knight; pages 119, 123 Paul Tyagi; page 127 Peter Durant; page 129 David Churchill; page 131 Anthony Weller; page 135 Simon Yeo; page 145 Peter Blundell Jones; page 147 Keith Hunter; page 149 Errol Forbes; page 153 Simon Morrison; page 155 Many Reynolds; page 157 Kee Photographic

Service Point

Service Point is again pleased to be associated with the Stirling Prize ceremony, as it is with the Centre for the Understanding of the Built Environment (CUBE) gallery in Manchester, together with Glasgow '99 and London Open House. Through the years, from our earliest years, as a drawing office, to our present position at the forefront of fully digital plan printing and electronic document management, the AEC and design community has been our world. We are thankful to be given the opportunity to put something back, thus helping to raise wider awareness of the impact that this community has on everyday life.

service point
DIGITAL REPROGRAPHICS   COMMUNICATIONS

More than 400 digitally connected locations nationally and internationally
Digital Reprographics, Printing, Copying, Imaging and Exhibition Graphics, Electronic Document Management, Facilities Management, Office products and Consumables, Integrated Services Solutions

MARKETING SERVICES 0800 634 24 24, www.pickingpack.net